The Vision Blueprint

8 Undeniable Principles to Successfully Executing Your Vision

VALERIE A. RICHARDSON, Ph.D

Copyright © 2020 by Valerie A. Richardson, Ph.D

All rights reserved. No part of this publication may be reproduced, distributed, or transmitted in any form or by any means, including photocopying, recording, or other electronic or mechanical methods, without the prior written permission of the publisher, except in the case of brief quotations embodied in critical reviews and certain other noncommercial uses permitted by copyright law. For permission requests, write to the publisher, addressed "Attention: Permissions Coordinator," at the address below.

Printed in the United States of America

To My Grandparents

Alexander and Melissa Richardson and Charlie and Glenis Landrew, for planting seeds of limitless potential within my DNA.

To My Rock, My Father

Earl L. Richardson, Sr.,
for teaching me the importance of hard work, having faith and compassion, and perseverance. I dedicate each word on the pages of this book and
every beat of my heart.

ACKNOWLEGEMENTS

I want to thank and honor my mother, Queen Nadine Landrew, for being the epitome of strength, grace, love, and tenacity. You have taught me the importance of loving, giving, nurturing, and helping others. I humbly acknowledge that I would not be the woman that I am today if it were not for you being the woman that you are.

I would like to thank Bishop Michael L. Smith for seeing and speaking the gift of writing into my life; and Pastor Eric A. Williams for covering, teaching, and praying for me.

Thanks to my special friends and family who pray for me, love, support, and encourage me to be all that God has created me to be.

I would also like to thank, Mr. Spec McClendon, who went home to be with the Lord a few weeks before the release of this book. He contributed to this book without hesitation and unbeknownst to him, he encouraged me spiritually and inspired me to pursue purpose and not prosperity. Yet, his life is a testament of how godliness and humility summon blessings.

"Your vision will become clear only when you look into your heart. Who looks outside, dreams; who looks inside, awakens."
-Carl Jung

Contents

Introduction..1

Principle 1:
Keep it Real...4

Principle 2:
Take a Selfie..16

Principle 3:
Know Your Worth..26

Principle 4:
Circle-Size Your Life...38

Principle 5:
"Mind" Your Business: "BOSS UP"............................48

Principle 6:
Pursue R & R (Research & Relationships).................61

Principle 7:
"Work" It..76

Principle 8:
Don't Give Up...95

Visionary's Corner..110

THE VISION BLUEPRINT

Introduction

Well, it's another year, and no matter if it's the beginning, middle, or end of the year, my question to you is "What have you done differently this year to bring the changes that you desire in your life?" What is the vision that you have for your life? You have probably attended more vision parties than you can think of over the years and have a multitude of vision boards. When are you going to decide to take those things off the vision board and bring them to life? Aren't you tired of talking about the changes that you want to see in your life, but nothing ever seems to change? Well, change happens when *you* change. You'll see something different only when you decide to do something different.

It's time for you to get off the shore and step into the water and take a chance on having the life you desire. What are those things that you dream and fantasize about? What are the things that you see yourself doing? What if I told you that you can do those things or that you can have those things if you would just make the decision today to step up, step out, and take a risk? What do you have to lose other than leaving your mediocre life and stepping into your best life?

Valerie A. Richardson, Ph.D

Your best life is whatever you desire it to be. It's what you envision it to be. Your vision is your vision, and it's up to you to pursue it. Your vision may simply be mending broken relationships, having the wedding of your dreams, blessing others, buying your dream home, patenting an invention, or having your own business. Whatever it is, it's time for you to execute it or enhance it. Every vision starts as a seed, thought or a picture in your mind. One fact about seeds is that they must germinate and be cultivated before they bring forth a harvest.

Without a vision, the people perish. God created each of us through His vision with purpose in mind. Vision and purpose are siblings. You were created with vision in your heart for purpose. Your purpose is identified through your passion and not necessarily your profession. Some of you may say that I know what my vision is and I'm walking in it now and that's awesome. However, the one thing about vision is that it's continual. You never stop seeing or visualizing things. It's a part of who we are. Purpose never dies. There will always be someone or something that needs you or the gifts and talents that you possess. So, no matter where you are in life, walking out your vision, renewing your vision, or trying to figure it out, I hope that this book will motivate, direct, equip and advance you where you need and desire to be.

Vision takes faith and work to bring forth the change you desire. It's time to stop letting fear, doubt, worry, uncertainty, low-self-esteem, and complacency keep you from fulfilling your vision and living your best life. It's time to stop settling for the job, the bad relationship, the apartment, living paycheck to paycheck, and settling in life when you saw much more for yourself. It's time to step out on faith and get moving. It's time to believe in yourself, to believe that you can do it, that you can have a better life. It's time to start living your best life now.

THE VISION BLUEPRINT

Your ideal life, or best life, may not be the same as someone else's, but whatever it is, it's time for you to pursue it and live it.

This book was birthed from my vision to see you liberated from dead, unfulfilled jobs, distractions, and responsibilities that deviate from the vision you have for your life. It was written to help deliver you from merely existing and move you into fully living by creating a life that's purpose and passion-driven. It was written to help you tap into who you really are and what you really want to do. It was written in hopes that you would be encouraged to use your God-given gifts, talents and abilities to execute your vision and bring self-fulfillment. It was written to help you realize that there is still time to make a U-turn and use this blueprint to lead you on your vision quest.

This book was written to help you realize that you are special and unique and that you have been given a vision on purpose. It's now time for you to find purpose in your vision and execute it with no excuses. This book will help you discover the real you, appreciate your value and worth, accept your past and encourage, empower, and equip you to step out into the future that you desire and deserve.

So don't let this year be about another boring, unproductive vision party, but make it the year that you mend the relationship, buy the house, fix your credit, lose the weight, make the investment, write the book or start the business, etc. This book was designed to help you to evaluate where you currently are and motivate you to start making steps to where you want to be. You don't have to wait until the next year. Your new year starts now, with you making the decision to change. It's time for you to step out and start taking the necessary steps toward change. If you decide to follow these eight principles to executing your vision, by this time next year, you'll be celebrating your progress, accomplishments and enjoying the fruits of your labor.

PRINCIPLE 1:
KEEP IT REAL

THE VISION BLUEPRINT

Principle 1: Keep It Real

Many times, you want to see change in your life, but you neglect to face the reality that change does not come by osmosis or through someone else. You may feel that the mere thought of change wills it into existence. You sense confession, elongated prayer, and even constant discussion of the change will trigger it to happen automatically, but that is typically not the case.

The reality is that change begins with YOU, and not with anyone or anything else in your life. Change starts by looking into the mirror and facing your reality. Oxford defines reality as "the state of things as they actually exist as opposed to an idealistic or notional idea of them."

So, my question to you is, "what is your reality?"

Accepting your reality may not be the easiest thing to do; in fact, it may be one of the most challenging things you have ever had to

Principle 1: Keep It Real

do. Why is that? Because accepting reality may cause you to face what you see in the mirror. It may cause you to have to revisit past and present life experiences or decisions. It may require you to self-reflect on who you are, where you came from, where you currently are, and why you are where you are today. It is not always easy to face your past mistakes, failures, personal disappointments, or current situations.

It is easier to avoid talking about where you are in your life, relationships, professions, and finances, instead of discussing where you could or should be. The difficulty stems from your fear that present realities may become your permanent actuality. Facing that possibility causes stress and worry, so instead, you choose to avoid it altogether. No one wants to imagine that their current, undesired reality might be their future.

In many cases, your current position mimics the discouraging realities of your family, friends, and environment. When this happens, the fretful thought of failure and defeat becomes real. For example, the concept of failed marriages, wayward children, being broke, living a defeated life with sickness and disease, settling for working a minimum wage paying job, and living in poverty becomes a perplexing reality.

It may seem hard to confront your life, but it's necessary. Acknowledging, accepting, understanding, and building from your reality can point you to a better future if *you desire change in your life. The good news is that your present experience does not have to be your definitive reality.* However, if you do not "Keep it Real" by acknowledging that your situation is what it is, you may become your own worst enemy and prevent yourself from having a better future.

THE VISION BLUEPRINT

Acknowledge Your Past to Change Your Future

Being real with yourself may be difficult because you may have to face some things that happened in your past that may be currently deterring your future. To move forward, you may have to revisit your pain. This action helps you to understand that *your pain ignites the passion that can push you into your purpose*. If you choose to continue to bury or ignore the pain, it often continues to cloud your vision and stagnate your progress. *Painful situations that you experience in life are not to break and destroy you but to perfect and grow you.* Your pain is a part of who you are, and you can use it to usher you into who you are purposed to be.

> ***Your pain can be used to ignite passion that can be used for a purpose.***

Know that you are not alone; we all have a past and a story to tell. All of us have encountered some painful things in life, but what differentiates us is how we choose to use the pain. *You can let it continue to persecute and paralyze you, or you can use it to progress and promote you.* Most time, vision is born through your pain. It is when you choose to be real about what you have gone through and how it has impacted you that you can move forward to having a better future. If you get trapped in the past, it will hinder your vision for your future.

If you are having problems coping with your past or present and you cannot seem to push past it, reach out for help. You have friends and family, other people, and resources that can help you work through your experiences. There are licensed counselors,

Principle 1: Keep It Real

psychiatrists, social workers, life coaches, support groups, and spiritual leaders that can help move you toward having a better life. You do not have to lodge in the pain because your future is greater than your pain. You can choose to seek help, work through it, and use it for a greater purpose.

You cannot allow pain and problems to decapitate you. Take back your power and reverse their intended effect. At some point in life, help is needed from someone you can trust and talk to about things that rudely interrupt or intercept your life. Seeking counsel and direction from others can help you to put things in perspective so you can move forward. Their assistance can help you realize how to turn things around and use your experiences for your good and the good of others. Your pain can be used intentionally to help someone else. My favorite scripture proclaims, "***And you know that all things work together for good to those who love the Lord and are called according to His purpose*** (Romans 8:28 New King James Version).

Yes, you may have been sexually abused, rejected, beaten, sick, imprisoned, abandoned, lied on, wrongfully accused, manipulated, deceived, etc. Richard Wright said, "***The impulse to dream has been slowly beaten out of me by experience.***"

You may not understand why it happened to you, and instead of dwelling on the *why*, pursue the *what*. What can you do with what has happened to you to get your dream back? You must push past the pity and attention-seeking state because if you don't, you may never work past what happened to you. *You must decide to use your experiences to help minimize or prevent it from happening to someone else.* Stop wallowing in sorrow and defeat and take back your power, your focus, and regain your vision for your life. What happened to you was only a setback for a set up in your future. So, be realistic about where you are, and acknowledge that you have an opportunity to change directions. James Baldwin said, **"Not everything that is faced can be changed, but nothing can be changed until it is faced."**

You must face your present and face your fears head-on if you want to see change. *If you do not acknowledge your current location, you may never make it to your expected destination*. When Google Maps does not have your current location, it is impossible to direct you to your desired destination. How would you know if you are headed in the wrong direction and need to make a U-turn if you never acknowledge your initial location?

Acknowledgment of your present position is not to cause you shame, fear, or stress. Ideally, it is to induce growth, redirection, and progression. It helps you strategize what it takes to move toward fulfilling your dreams and goals. Knowing your present reality encourages you to make different, challenging

> *If you don't acknowledge your current location, you may never make it to your expected destination.*

decisions that will help change the course of your life. Facing your reality and keeping it real can be life changing.
You can make necessary changes right now that will redirect the course of your life and lead you where you desire to be. So even though you may be living in the present, you can still ***THINK and BELIEVE in your future.*** You can begin to see and meditate on what you want your life to be. You can change the direction and perception in your mind and start seeing yourself living in what

Principle 1: Keep It Real

you desire.

When you can think about what you desire and *believe* in it, then you will *see* and *live* it. **Your reality begins to change the moment your perception changes.** You must continuously speak to yourself and believe that your situation is changing and commit to taking the necessary steps to implement that change.

Change and vision require making sacrifices that may be uncomfortable and stretch you out of the norm. They both force you to work tirelessly and faithfully. That is what it takes to point the compass of your reality towards your desired destination.

Accept Responsibility

The time has come to accept that your reality is what it is partially due to decisions or lack thereof. Whether your choices were intentional or unintentional, the reality is that you made a choice. Even if the decision you made was not to decide, it still caused corresponding consequences, whether positive or negative. Since you made the decisions, you must accept that the results are yours to bear. That is why it compels you to think long and hard before you make decisions as it relates to your personal life and well-being. Life-altering choices such as who you will marry, who and what you believe in, if you will go to college, what career you will choose, and whether you will be an employer or employee are all decisions that require serious thought and prayer. Be mindful that every decision you make yields a result that will affect your life temporarily or permanently.

Typically, the decisions that yield good outcomes will encourage repeated actions and direct your future choices. In retrospect, the same applies to decisions that you have made that resulted in unfavorable effects. Because of the consequences of your actions, you are now more cautious about duplicating those preferences. Although, you know some decisions caused you to experience adverse endings; you may still find yourself repeating the same actions and making the same choices. Generally, this occurs when you are afraid of *stepping out* of your comfort zone, thus causing your reality to remain the same.

Your current state not only results from your decisions but also your environment. Wonder why you are where you are presently in life? The answer is simple; it is where you have chosen to reside. You say you want more money, a better relationship, or your own business, etc. However, you find yourself in the same situation weeks, months, and even years later. What is keeping you from moving forward? Could it be that you have not been real with yourself about where you are and that *you* are the primary obstacle standing in the way of your anticipated reality?

You can decide today to do things differently and change your destiny. It is time to get out of your comfort zone. Greg Pitt said it best, **"Your comfort zone is your danger zone."**

It is time to face your fears and turn your dreams into reality. You must realize that you played a significant part in your present, and you also have the power to decide to shift things forward towards your desired future.

Your breakthrough of change begins when you acknowledge that it is time to change your reality. Les Brown said, **"What if you lived your whole life and discovered that it was wrong, that you were chosen to do something else, and you didn't do it?**

If your life does not resemble what you pictured, it is time to start making decisions that will lead you to where you desire to be. The time has come to pursue a career and apply for the job. Walk-in boldness and leave the bad relationship. Exercise initiative and go back to school, apply for the loan, place the bid for the house, commit to the relationship, start the business, and be your *best you*. You are just a decision away from turning your life around and

Principle 1: Keep It Real

walking in your vision.

It is easy to play the blame game and point fingers at others, or your past for where you are in life. Yes, your parent's decisions, your upbringing, and your environment contributed an integral part in your present condition. However, you cannot dismiss the fact that you have also played a sizable part in creating your current world. The good news is you are the driving force and pivotable player in changing your domain.

> *"What if you lived your whole life and discovered that it was wrong, that you were chosen to do something else, and you didn't do it?"*
> **-Les Brown**

The path to change your reality requires you to revisit your past and accept your present. The voyage begins when you decide to change your future.

Therefore, you need to ask yourself some real, yet difficult but necessary questions. Your answers will catapult you into the life you envisioned. It is one thing to be pretentious with others, but your demise to be artificial with yourself. Keep it real with yourself when responding so that you can pinpoint exactly where you are and what steps you need to take to redirect your life where you desire to be.

THE VISION BLUEPRINT

REFLECTIONS

What past decisions are affecting your present reality? Answer for each area in your life (health, career, spiritual, personal, etc.).

How has (is) your environment affected your desired reality?

Who in your environment is affecting your current and desired reality? How are they affecting it?

What can you do to make your environment more conducive to achieving your desired reality?

What current decisions are you making that are affecting the changes that you desire in life (health, career, spiritual, personal, etc.)?

What decisions do you need to make to change your present reality to lead you where you want to be (health, career, spiritual, personal, etc.)?

Principle 1: Keep It Real

PRAYER OF INSPIRATION

Lord, I realize that I have a past, and many things have happened in my life from childhood throughout my adulthood. But I realize that you make no mistakes, and your Word says that you predestined my life before the very foundation of the world; and that you knew me even before I was in my mother's womb. You have plans for me and my life. Thank you that nothing in my life is a surprise to you. Please help me to understand that it all had to happen, and it was all necessary to make me into the person that I am today. Help me to understand that it will all be used to perfect me. Your Word says in II Corinthians 4:8-18 that even though we are troubled on every side, we are not distressed; we are perplexed, but not in despair; we may be persecuted, but I thank you that I am not forsaken, and I may be cast down, but I'm not destroyed. Thank you that nothing that has happened in my life has destroyed me, but it has all been used to perfect me for the great future that you have in store for me. Thank you for using everything in my life to build me and not break me. You told us that in this world, we will have trials and tribulations, but to be of good cheer because you have overcome this world and therefore, so shall I. Therefore, help me to trust that you are working everything that has happened good or bad in my life for my good because I love you and I am chosen for your purpose. Increase my faith to speak and believe for my desired reality. Help me to be real with myself and to make the necessary changes and steps that I need to take for me to see what I desire and what you have purposed for my life. Help me to be real with myself so that I can encourage others to be real with

THE VISION BLUEPRINT

themselves and to follow the blueprint of vision to purpose and lodge in destiny. In Jesus' name, Amen!

Principle 2: Take a Selfie

PRINCIPLE 2:
TAKE A SELFIE

Principle 2: Take A Selfie

Do you ever feel like there is something else that you should be doing with your life? Are there times when you notice that your mind is migrating into several differing directions? For example, you may think it is a good idea to open a daycare because you like children, or that you should be an educator because you enjoy teaching. You might also consider opening a burger joint because you believe that you make the best burgers. You may even find yourself having the urge to do something simply because someone else has proven to be effective at achieving it.

Several ideas consume your thoughts but, yet you seem to remain unclear on where to begin or what to do. The uncertainty of what you should do may originate from peer or social pressures, or unconsciously competing and comparing yourself with others. For

Principle 2: Take a Selfie

instance, you may compare yourself to a friend who gained notoriety for a successful daycare, to an associate that received an award for teacher of the year, or to a burger joint owner that earned recognition for the Best Burger in the South. You may feel anxious to compete with society's moguls by feeling pressured to write the next New York Times bestseller, start the next Fortune 500 Company, be the next Steve Jobs, Les Brown, Steve Bezos, or Oprah Winfrey. Sadly, these anxieties heighten the confusion of who you really are and desire to be.

Identity is defined as the distinguishing character or personality of an individual; individuality; the relation established by psychological identification (Identity," 2020). **Identity describes and reveals who you are.** It exposes what you like and dislike, makes you smile, makes you sad, makes you love, burdens or gives you peace, your thoughts about life and death, and your feelings about why you exist, etc. Identity reveals your uniqueness, morals, values, thoughts, and your perceived purpose. *Identity is and should be what separates you from everyone else.*

Self-identity is often confused with societal identity which contributes to disillusionment with who you are and who others think you should be. This confusion causes you to attempt to fit into society's mold by projecting the views, voices, and actions of those you deem significant and successful upon yourself. Then, naturally, your personal views become blurry, your voice begins to sound like someone else, and your actions begin to spawn from the directives of people that you are encouraged or pressured to duplicate.

The problem is that societal identity can potentially redefine your self-identity. These perceptions place stressors on you, who you are, and what makes you feel relevant, significant, and successful. Whereas, who you truly are is the opposite of society's labels and expectations. Therefore, this truth leads to the question of your authenticity. **Authenticity exposes your truths.** It divulges whether your speech and actions align with who you are versus who society, friends, and family expect you to be. Authenticity is about not pretending or forcing yourself to be someone that you are not. The danger of being unauthentic warps your sense of passion and purpose, and it leads you on a crooked path or destination other than what God planned for your life.

Erik Erikson believed that identity forms over time, throughout cycles of life. He coined the term "ego identity," which focused on a revolving sense of self (Levesque, 2001).

Ego identity expresses the importance of you focusing on all aspects of yourself. For example, it encompasses who you are as a friend, parent, professional, sibling, spiritually, etc. Ego identity explicates that even though you may serve in different capacities of life, everything that you do should still evolve from your true, authentic character. Although your roles may change, your core beliefs, morals, and values should remain unwavering. If they vary, you may not know who you are, or maybe you are not being true to yourself. As you mature, the calamities of life and the need for identity achievement may also cause you to reassess or redefine your values, priorities, significance, and identity. Aging and life experiences can also make you question who you really are, who you are meant to be, and who you ultimately see yourself becoming.

> *Authenticity exposes our truths.*

Principle 2: Take a Selfie

Who Are You?

Unfortunately, the reality is that if you do not realize "who you are," your forward progression in life can suffer. Identity issues lead to confusion on what you should do, which can produce complacency and dissatisfaction. You will find yourself in a frustrating place of discontentment when you envisioned more for your life. Yet, you remain puzzled and paralyzed because you are unclear on what to do.

There is an inner struggle of what you visualize yourself doing versus what others expect you to do. You must silence *society's voice and those around you and listen to the guidance in your heart and your spirit*. It is vital to discover your true vision and purpose. You need to take a self-examination of your likes and dislikes, your beliefs, values, innermost thoughts, secret meditations, dreams, and fantasies. It is necessary that you evaluate who you are and what you deem as important and valuable in life. You must find self-fulfillment and meaning by focusing on, executing, and accomplishing things that give you inner peace, a sense of belonging, purpose, and accomplishment.

Fulfillment does not come when you are doing what others want you to do; it only comes when you satisfy your passion in life. Therefore, you should **take the time to discover yourself so that you can become yourself**. It is time to take an inner selfie- and stop focusing on the external, filtered, polished selfies that you post on social media. *The inner selfie exposes the real, unfiltered, authentic you.* Only then will you discover yourself and begin to move forward in executing those things that define you with passion and determination. Focus on things that you find yourself doing with ease that bring you a sense of true identity, fulfillment, accomplishment, and peace. **When you discover who you truly are, you uncover why you exist.**

THE VISION BLUEPRINT

Discover Your Vision

YOUR vision is an extension of your very existence, your gifts, talents, thoughts, morals, values, personality, dreams, passion, compassion, heart, etc. When your vision does not coincide with these things, it may not be *your* vision, but someone else's. *A misguided vision is just as detrimental as having no vision and merely existing.* It causes you to go in circles with no defined goals or established destinations. It can deceive you into believing that someone else's vision belongs to you. Attempting to fulfill a vision that is not yours can be confusing and challenging. Unfortunately, you could never successfully execute what is not in your heart. Your vision is that thing that lives inside you, that you cannot seem to shake. It forever shows up in your thoughts, dreams, and prayers. It is the thing you know in your heart no one can do like you because no one can beat you at being you.

> *A misguided vision is just as detrimental as having no vision and merely existing.*

So, how can you recognize if it is truly your vision or not? That is simple:

- It's that thing that you have thought about as a child.
- It's that thing that you have dreamed and fantasized about.
- It's that thing that you've always seen yourself doing.
- It's that thing that burdens your heart.
- It's that thing that you do with ease.
- It's that thing that gives you a sense of peace.
- It's that thing that separates you from everyone else.
- It's that thing that gives you purpose and self-fulfillment.
- It's that thing that you would do even if you did not get paid for it.

Principle 2: Take a Selfie

- It's that thing that helps you to help someone else.
- It's YOUR VISION.

YOU ARE YOUR VISION. *Your vision will always coincide with who you are, and you will always coincide with your vision.* If you want to know who you really are and if you are staying true to yourself, your calling, and fulfilling your destiny, ask yourself some tough yet revealing questions. Once you discover your true, authentic self, then it becomes easy to pursue and execute your vision and to find peace, purpose, and fulfillment in it.

> ***Take time to discover yourself so that you can become yourself.***

THE VISION BLUEPRINT

REFLECTIONS

What do you tend to find fulfillment in doing?

What don't you like to do?

What are your hobbies?

Which job(s) have you had that you like? Dislike?

Do you feel fulfilled with what you are doing now? If not, what would you like to be doing now?

What would you do even if you did not get paid for it?

What makes you smile? What makes you sad?

What are your gifts? Talents? Abilities?

What are your beliefs? Values?

What do you do that comes natural with little to no effort?

What do you do well that people are willing to pay you to do?

What is difficult for you to do?

If you were given the finances and opportunity to do anything right now, what would it be?

After answering these questions, now ask yourself, what do you think your purpose is?

Principle 2: Take a Selfie

Do you think you are currently walking in vision? If not, it is time to follow this blueprint and take the necessary steps that you need to take to get on the road to executing your vision/purpose.

PRAYER OF INSPIRATION

Lord, please show me and help me to see what you have invested and instilled on the inside of me. Help me to clearly see the vision that you have given me. Help me to silence the voice of others, what they think I should be doing or who they think I am. Help me to get outside of the box and not let anyone put me in a box any longer. Help me to see and know my purpose and destiny. Help me to follow my vision and my purpose. Let me not miss your leading and your voice but let me be guided by your Spirit. Let me not be misled by following money, titles, positions, or others, but help me to follow the desires that you have given me in my heart. Give me the vision and purpose that you have for MY Life, and give me the wisdom, knowledge, understanding, resources, and people to fulfill it. Help me to see myself how you see me in spite of my imperfections. Help me to see the gifts, talents, and abilities that you've given me and help me to put those God-given qualities to use to help someone else see and find themselves. Help me to be vision-minded and see and be the best me that I can be for Your Glory and the good of your people. In Jesus' name, Amen.

Principle 3: Know Your Worth

PRINCIPLE 3:
KNOW YOUR WORTH

THE VISION BLUEPRINT

Principle 3: Know Your Worth

Do you ever find yourself comparing your thoughts and actions to those of others? Are you internally competing with those around you? How about mimicking someone else's hair, walk, talk, occupation, and lifestyle? Have you unconsciously coveted and compared yourself to someone else's friends, relationships, occupation, network, and net worth?

When asked who you are, do you identify yourself by your job title or position? Would your responses sound something like the following?

"I'm Jane Doe from the President's office."

"I'm Jane Doe, Nurse Practitioner."

"I'm Elder Jane Doe, from First Baptist International Love Missionary Covenant Believers Church of God in Christ."

Principle 3: Know Your Worth

"I'm Jane Doe, owner of Identity Crisis, Incorporated."

"I'm Jane Doe, Dr. Somebody's daughter."

The question was not who you were employed by or affiliated with, nor what is your job title; it was "Who are you?" A simple response to that question would be "I'm Jane Doe," without mentioning any other person, positions, or titles.

So, the ultimate question is, why do you feel the need to identify yourself by giving your positions or mentioning your connections? May I submit to you that it is because you are not confident in your identity and self-worth. Therefore, you often find yourself referencing titles and affiliations when asked who you are. By doing so, you *equate your self-worth to job titles, relationships, social networks, and net worth. While minimizing your worthiness, you diminish the vastness of who you are.* When you truly know your self-worth, you will respond by simply saying, "Hi, I'm Jane Doe."

The response is humble yet laden because it displays confidence in who you are. It exudes your self-worth, uniqueness, boldness, and versatility. You are saying, I may not be a doctor, president, CEO, or pastor, but I still have gifts, talents, and abilities. You are declaring, "I am Jane Doe, I am significant, I am somebody, and I have something to offer."

Self-worth is defined as the sense of one's value or worth as a person; self-esteem, self-respect ("Self-worth," 2020). Unfortunately, you are practicing leaving out the word "self" in self-worth and focusing on the word 'worth." Doing this allows a broad spectrum of measuring for your worth against someone else or what society coins as worthy while not appreciating your intrinsic value. Society's competitive trends may lead to distorted views. These trends may cause you to believe that if your titles, affiliations, or finances are not in the above-average brackets, you are not valuable, and do not have much to offer. In turn, this causes you to compare yourself to others and gradually diminish your self-worth and repeatedly mimic the values, occupation, appearance, position, and purpose of others.

Constantly comparing your value to someone else leads to an ongoing internal war of assuming that you are not good enough. The comparison will cause you to believe that you must continually strive to be as great as someone else instead of just being the best "you" that you can be. *The reality is that you will never win at trying to satisfy others or being someone other than you because you can only be "you."* There will always be someone wiser, more affluent, slimmer, more athletic, more talented, more beautiful, or more spiritual. Why continue the cycle of trying to be someone other than yourself? Only when you focus on becoming your best self, will you discover your true worth and value.

The Word of God reveals that you are shaped in the image and likeness of God (Genesis 1:27 New King James Version). It explains that you are fearfully and wonderfully made (Psalm 139:14 New King James Version); and before God formed you in your mother's womb, He knew you (Jeremiah 1:5 New King James Version). It further discloses that your life was predestined even before the very foundation of the world (Ephesians 1:4 New King James Version). Therefore, the establishment of your worth took form in your creation with your purpose in mind. You are individually formed and made by God, and that is why you purposely have a distinct DNA, fingerprint, appearance, and vision.

> *We were all created with a purpose in mind.*

Principle 3: Know Your Worth

Different to Make a Difference

Being different is not a curse; it is a blessing. Even identical twins have similar yet different fingerprints. Though they may have the same DNA, their appearance and personalities are uniquely different. Therefore, God never intended for anyone to be exactly alike, but to be different because we all have a different purpose and assignment. We all have something different to contribute to society and life. Together, our gifts, personalities, talents, professions, experiences, tragedies, thoughts, and upbringing, all make us the inimitable human beings that we are.

Your self-worth increases when you realize that there is only one you, and there is no one who will ever be you. **People may be able to imitate you, but they will never be able to duplicate you.** *Self-worth increases with the realization that the value of something increases with its rarity, and there is none other like it.* For example, the rarer a diamond is, the more valuable it is. Of all colored diamonds, red diamonds are the rarest; therefore, it is considered most valuable. Since red diamonds are so treasured, society expects that we should all be red diamonds, or our value diminishes. The problem with that philosophy is that not every diamond carries the hue or the same elements that are needed to become a red diamond. However, that does not change the fact that it is still a diamond. Therefore, the reality is that every diamond will never become a red diamond. What they can become is the best blue, white, yellow, or black diamond that they can be. Each diamond is valuable and has a purpose for its color and its use. Different people may prefer different types of diamonds for varying reasons, which is how they all serve an individual purpose. Just like diamonds, you are unique and valuable in your own right, and you have an individual vision and an assignment to fulfill. You have different characteristics because you have a distinct group of people to serve and assist. Your exclusive

THE VISION BLUEPRINT

personal life experiences, resources, and skills will help you to accomplish certain tasks and fulfill your purpose.

You are God's most prized possession. He has invested a lot in you, and He expects a return on His investment. You must realize that He invested in you on purpose and for a purpose. The purpose was so you could invest in someone else. So, if you are reading this book, know that you are valuable, and *there is something extraordinary about you that is impossible to imitate.* Know that the universe needs your uniqueness, gifts, and your talents. You are significant, and what you have to offer is priceless. However, you will never realize your self-worth if you continue to validate your worth by society's grid or through the eyes of someone else. When you recognize that the only measuring stick that you should measure yourself against is the one that you have set for yourself and the one that God has placed in your heart, then you will begin to comprehend the immensity of your self-worth.

You must understand the importance of your self-worth, in doing so, you will discover that you have something to offer society. Stop letting people define you and keep you in a box. Unfortunately, when you do not believe in your self-worth, there is a greater risk that you will not step out to pursue your greater self and vision. *The discovery of your worth begins with your inner thoughts of self-confidence and consciousness of your God-given abilities.*

Jane Doe may not be the next Michelle Obama, Alice Walton, or Oprah Winfrey, but she needs to believe that she can be the best version of herself that she can be. She needs to know that what she has to offer matters, that she can make a difference, and add value to someone's life. She must believe that she can say something that might help someone or that she can do something that may change a life or impact the world.

When you limit your uniqueness by comparing yourself to others, you tend not to pursue your greatness. Instead, you find yourself

Principle 3: Know Your Worth

disappointed, unproductive, and pointlessly competitive. Trying to mimic your peers only causes internal and external frustrations, which eventually leads to failure. You will never succeed in trying to be someone else. You should embrace your God-given gifts and talents and seek ways to display your uniqueness and abilities to impact the lives of others.

To pursue and accomplish great things, you must know that you are worthy of doing great things. Yes, YOU have value, YOU are PRICELESS, YOU have gifts and talents like NO ONE else, YOU have creative ideas like NO ONE else, YOU are unique, and YOU are YOU. When you know your self-worth, others will believe in you, what you have to say and what you have to offer. It does not matter where you have come from or where you have been, nor what you have been through, you are still worthy. *Where you have been and what you have gone through makes you the inimitable person that you are. Use your experiences to make you and someone else better and not bitter. Don't allow life encounters to paralyze you, but to perfect, promote, and push you into your destiny.*

> **People may be able to imitate you, but they will never be able to duplicate you.**

THE VISION BLUEPRINT

You Are Still Worthy

Oprah Winfrey was born in the small, impoverished state of Mississippi. She was molested as a child and became pregnant at age 14. She lost her child to premature death (Knatt, 2014). Nevertheless, she became a billionaire philanthropist and is now considered one of the most influential women in America. Tyler Perry, raised in New Orleans, Louisiana, experienced child abuse, homelessness, and earned only a GED (Buchel, 2019). That said, he is now a renowned billionaire, writer, producer, director, and entrepreneur. He has built an empire that consists of successful films, plays, sitcoms, and drama series. Just in case some of you still are not convinced that no matter what you have gone through, you are still worthy of vision, then let me help you.

Steve Jobs, the founder of Apple, was an adopted college dropout (Knatt, 2014). In 2018 his company became one of the world's first trillion-dollar businesses (Heath, 2018). Even in death, his legacy continues because he did not allow his past insufficiencies to define or diminish who he was and what he had to offer. He believed in himself enough to step out, exercise his gifts, talents, and abilities while executing his vision. Joyce Meyers was mentally, emotionally, verbally, and sexually abused by her father, but she realized and embraced her self-worth (Ducille, 2020). She exercised her uniqueness and is now a New York Times best-selling author of several books, and a world-renowned televangelist (Ducille, 2020). Now, hopefully, you get the picture. These icons are ordinary people, just like you and me. They all experienced challenging situations, yet decided to believe that they were worthy, they were significant, and had something to offer to society. They decided to push past their negative experiences, believe in themselves, and execute their vision. As a result of their belief, they have impacted the lives of millions.

Just like these influencers, you have had challenging life experiences, encountered obstacles, and barriers. These incidences have caused you to question your self-worth and ability to be great

Principle 3: Know Your Worth

while reaching your full potential. Just as these moguls overcame their insurmountable circumstances and did not allow their situations to devalue their worth and capabilities, neither should you. **Overcoming challenges demonstrates that your value is not assessed by your past, nor by obstacles. You can only become what you believe you can become. You can only do what you BELIEVE that you can do. Knowing your self-worth is WORTH it.** *You* are valuable. *You* have a gift, and *you* are a gift. *You* have something to offer; *you* have something that someone else needs. Someone is waiting for *you* to believe in *yourself* and execute your vision to motivate them to believe in themselves so they can execute their vision.

Stop comparing yourself to others and realize that your gifts, abilities, and talents are distinctive. Your value is still like that of the red diamond. Even if your hue can only produce blue diamonds; you are still a diamond. Once you realize your true self-worth, you will be ready to share who you are, your desires, passion, and abilities. Then you will eagerly execute your vision so you can encourage and help others to initiate their vision. Execution of your vision only happens when you know who you are, know your worth, and are confident in what you have to offer.

It was not until I read the Bible and "Woman Thou Art Loosed," by Bishop T.D. Jakes, that I began to discover who God made me to be. I began to understand who I was and how precious I was to God. It helped me discover that God wonderfully made me on purpose. Therefore, I must be all that to God! I finally realized that I was perfectly imperfect and wonderfully made by God. He precisely intended to make me *"on purpose for a purpose."*

So, if God saw me as perfectly imperfect, and valuable, then why shouldn't I see myself as the same? *What gave me or anyone else the right to devalue what God had already valued?* Both books changed me. They changed the direction and course of my life. They delivered me from negative thinking to believing in who God was in me and who I was in Him. I began to see that I am special and chosen by God, even in the midst of all of my mistakes. I realized that I am all that, in God, with God, and for God. Self-worth is not arrogance. I gained confidence in knowing and believing that God makes no mistakes; and he uniquely created you and me for His glory and the good of others.

To successfully execute your vision, you must fully understand your self-worth and value to God and others. It helps to take a close examination of yourself, who you are, what makes you unique and what you have to offer to others and society. You must appreciate who you are and know that there is greatness in YOU, and God has glorious works for YOU to accomplish. To do this, you must ask yourself some thoughtful yet revealing questions and meditate on what makes you unique.

Answering these questions will help you to understand both your worth and value. Each response will force you off the shore and into the water, where you will begin executing your vision and becoming your best self.

> *You can only become what you believe you can become. You can only do what you BELIEVE that you can do. Knowing your self-worth is WORTH it.*

Principle 3: Know Your Worth

REFLECTIONS

Define self-worth.

How do you view your self-worth? What does God say about your worth?

Who and what have you allowed to define your worth?

What do you need to do to realize your self-worth?

What gifts, talents, and abilities contribute to your self-worth?

How can your life's experiences be used to contribute to your value?

How can the realization of your self-worth help someone else?

What have you learned about your overall self-worth? How do you plan to use this new revelation to execute and/or enhance your vision?

THE VISION BLUEPRINT

PRAYER OF INSPIRATION

Lord, please help me to recognize that I am your creation and your child and that you have made me in your very own image and likeness. Help me to realize that your scripture says that I am fearfully and wonderfully made by you, that I am carved in the palm of your hand, and that I am the apple of your eye with all of my imperfections. Thank you for reminding me that simply because you made me and created me for your purpose, I am special and worthy of a productive life of prosperity, peace, and joy. I am grateful that your Word says that you came that I might have life and have it more abundantly. Thank you for reminding me that I have value and that it is my purpose to add value to others and remind them of their worth. Thank you for loving me and choosing me to represent you here on the Earth, and for trusting me to fulfill your purpose for my life. Please remind me daily who I am in you and that you have made me unique and chosen me for greater works. Help me to always remember my worth and to stay humble in the midst of it. Help me to remember that I am chosen, special and royal because I was made by you for a purpose on purpose. Help me to see myself the way you see me and to believe that I am worthy simply because you said I am. Help me to believe in myself and give me the strength and faith to execute the vision that you have given me. In Jesus Name, Amen!

PRINCIPLE 4:
CIRCLE-SIZE YOUR LIFE

THE VISION BLUEPRINT

Principle 4: Circle-Size Your Life

Your environment can influence your thinking, reality, and vision productivity. Your atmosphere can mold your beliefs, values, health, career, and success. Unconsciously, your surroundings affect your world more than you realize. You are a social being that craves the need for social acceptance. Your natural and cultural environments influence you. For example, your cultural environment affects who you are, and your natural environment influences your mental and physical status. Your atmosphere shapes your overall being. For instance, if an Asian child were born in Asia, but raised in the United States, that child would primarily take on the culture and language of an American, not an Asian. This scenario is indicative of an environment-behavior correlation. It insinuates your environment can innately affect your thinking and behaviors positively or negatively.

You Are Your Circle

Other things that directly influence your environment are people surrounding you. Let me prove it to you by asking these questions.

Principle 4: Circle-Size Your Life

Have you ever found yourself saying or doing things that you have never said or done before?

Have you ever found yourself mimicking those around you?

Have you ever heard a friend/companion singing a song or saying a slogan, and you find yourself repeating the same song or slogan?

Your environment is inclusive of the people around you because they can directly or indirectly influence your decisions and, ultimately, your life. For this reason, you must select and monitor those with whom you associate. It is essential that you pay attention to the words and actions of those around you because the direction of your life depends on it. You must ask yourself:

Do those who surround me inspire me to speak better, see better, and do better?

Do those around me encourage me to step out on faith to fulfill my vision?

Are those around me go-getters, catalysts, world changers, role models, encouragers, or motivators?

Do those around me push and inspire me to be great?

Do they show me tough love and correct me when I am wrong?

Do they force me to look at the man in the mirror, and to say and do the right thing?

Do they encourage me to be the best that I can be and not settle?

Do they tell me "No" when it is for my good?

THE VISION BLUEPRINT

Do they push me to have faith, be strong, stand, and believe that I can and will succeed in the face of opposition?

Do they possess the ability to teach me something that I do not know?

Are you surrounded by someone who can lead you where you want to go? Are you surrounded by those who have fallen but gotten up and succeeded? Are you surrounded by those who have failed but used failure as fuel to strategize future opportunities?

If you answered "no" to any of these questions, it may be time for you to circle-size your life and perform a "*circlecision.*" "***Circle-size" means to cut off those from your circle who negatively affect you, do not add value to you, or influence you to be your best self.*** You need to surround yourself with those who will push you in the water yet jump in and save you if they must in order for you to succeed. It is important to circle yourself with those who encourage you to get out of your comfort zone. Group yourself with those who nudge you to live life with no regrets, push past every obstacle with perseverance and faith, and not to take "No" for an answer.

It is best to gravitate around those that can help you develop and execute your vision. Surround yourself with those who inspire you, but also correct you, teach you, finance you, help you, motivate, and support you. When executing your vision, center yourself with others who also have a vision. It helps to be around people who are not just existing; but are walking, pursuing, or living in their own vision.

> *"Circle-size" simply means to cut off those from your circle who negatively affect you, don't add value to you or influence you to be your best self.*

Principle 4: Circle-Size Your Life

Evil Company Affects Good Behaviors

Your view and opinion of yourself has a lot to do with those around you. ***You will only go and grow as far as your company and environment allow***. You must avoid or dismiss people who are needy and drain you. Avoid those who always have issues and need a lot of time and attention. Avoid those who do not seem to support you yet hinder, criticize, or discourage you. Avoid those who have weak faith and blurred vision. If you continue to migrate around them, their negative thinking and need for attention will transfer to you, impeding your progress and success.

We have all heard the saying, "sticks and stones may break my bones, but words will never hurt me." I think that is one of the biggest lies ever told. Words are life, and they have the power to make you or break you. You must have people around you that speak life and add value to you. It is also vital that you have people around you that have a vision and direction for their own lives. Those same individuals need to be faithful people who see no limits and strive daily to reach higher heights.

Additionally, they need to be the type of go-getters who are executionists who establish results. You should surround yourself with those who see an open door in the middle of a mountain. It is necessary to be encircled by motivators, encouragers, and innovators. Visionaries should have people around them who are like-minded individuals and living examples of who they are or aspire to be. Place people in your circle who have a plan and are busy working that plan, because they are more likely to encourage you to do the same.

> ***You will only go and grow as far as your company and environment allows.***

THE VISION BLUEPRINT

Guard Your Gates

Your circle of influence also encompasses what you meditate on, see, and hear.

Do you find yourself being envious or fantasizing that other's lives were yours?

Do you wish you were married, had a significant other, traveled the world over, or had your own business as you have noticed with others?

Do you spend several hours a day scrolling on Facebook, Instagram, Snap Chat, Twitter, or Tik Tok to see what is going on in someone else's life?

Well, I hate to be the bearer of bad news, but most of what is said or posted on social media are fantasy posts. People tend to pretend and embellish the truth for personal validity, societal acceptance, or attention. The choice is yours; you could spend several wasted hours on fake media, or you could spend time working on executing your God-given vision.

The flip side is that positive social media posts can potentially have an invigorating effect on your vision. Optimistic posts can be used as inspiration to be better and do better by seeing that others are pursuing their goals and executing their visions. Progressive realities can encourage you to begin moving toward your goals. Constructive social media content is useful in offering networking opportunities to guide or connect you with resources or people. Those influences can lead you in the right direction toward fulfilling your goals. I advise you to glean from the positive that is posted on social media and dismiss the negative.

Please do not allow the confident, successful posts to intimidate you but permit them to motivate you. Let them inspire you to believe that if someone else did it, so can you. Be mindful,

Principle 4: Circle-Size Your Life

however, of the hours you are spending on social media. Limit media time and only use it as a positive reinforcement to execute your vision. The 2018 Nielsen Total Audience Report found that Americans spend more than 11 hours per day watching TV, reading, listening, or interacting with media. This number is up from the 9 hours reported in 2014. The Nielsen report also found that 64% of Smartphone users view social media at least once a day, which has risen to 72% with those 18-34 years of age. Being that research shows that our environment influences and engages us in media almost half the day, it behooves you to use media to encourage, motivate, and profit you. Use social media as a resource to discover information that enhances your knowledge and inspires you to initiate and cultivate your vision. Any media time outside of that can be a waste of vision time.

You must also be mindful of what circles your ears. Faith and motivation also come through hearing. The more motivational words and speakers, inspiring podcasts, tv programs, and e-books you hear, the more you are encouraged to walk in your vision. **Faith comes by hearing and doing something continually.** Therefore, you must always listen to encouraging things and people. You must avoid negative things and people because it can have a paralyzing effect, and cause your vision to be stagnated, misguided, or destroyed. Therefore, *anyone in your circle, speaking negative words of doubt and discouragement concerning your vision must be circle-sized.*

Words have power and life. Those around you can speak life or death into your vision. **Never allow anyone to have that much control over what you see and believe for your own life.** You must silence the mouth of those that speak pessimistically by removing them from your inner circle. In some instances, you will have to inform people if they are not speaking constructive, life-filled words around you, your interaction with them must cease. What others around you say or think about you will affect your world, productivity, and vision. However, you must remain grateful that you and God have governing authority concerning your life.

THE VISION BLUEPRINT

What are you saying about your life… about yourself? What do you believe about yourself? **What you believe about yourself is what you will become. Whatever you think about yourself enters your heart; whatever enters your heart, comes out of your mouth; and whatever comes out of your mouth leads to corresponding actions. Sometimes you have to circle-size yourself.** No, you cannot alienate yourself from yourself, but you have the power to cut off your negative, doubtful thoughts, words, and actions. It is critical that you practice speaking words of affirmation and motivation about who you are and what you can and will do.

Take time to evaluate those in your circle and what they are saying or demonstrating to you. Your observations will reveal if it is time to circle-size people or things in your life so that you can successfully execute your vision.

Principle 4: Circle-Size Your Life

REFLECTIONS

What do your friends, associates, companions, and family talk about in your presence?

What are your friends, associates, and family typically doing when you are around them?

What have you learned or gained from being around each of them?

How do you feel when you are around each of them?

What have you accomplished since you have been around them?

What are you doing when you find yourself around them?

Have they been more of a positive or negative influence in your life? Make a list of all the positive and negative influences of each person in your life.

What correction or guidance have each one of them given you?

How did they respond when you were on the mountain top and in the valley seasons of your life?

PRAYER OF INSPIRATION

Lord, please help me to recognize those people in my life that should not be there. Expose them for who they are and make their purpose and intentions known concerning me. Reveal to me every secret and hidden agenda of those around me that mean me no good. Help me to dismiss them from my life. Even those that I am close to and those difficult to disconnect from, I ask that you remove them if they do not have my best interest at heart. Cause them to dismiss themselves and never to return. Help me to recognize those in my life that mean me well and help me to gravitate closer to them and to bless them as you bless me. Please divinely connect me to those who are a part of my destiny and to those who will help me fulfill the vision that you have given me. Help those in my circle to see what you have shown me and who you have made me; and give them that same passion and drive to work, pray, and give toward my vision. Send people to encourage me when I get discouraged and to push me to keep going when I want to give up and help me to do the same for them. Send prayer warriors and those with financial and material resources to help me fulfill my calling and purpose for your glory and the good of your people. Help me to circle size my thoughts and actions and to speak only positive words of faith concerning my vision and the plans that you have for me. In Jesus Name, Amen!

Principle 5: "Mind" Your Business: "Boss Up"

PRINCIPLE 5:
"MIND" YOUR BUSINESS: "BOSS UP"

Principle 5: "Mind" Your Business; "Boss Up"

When you are ready to see and make a change in your life, your ingenuity fires on all cylinders, and you find yourself daydreaming ceaselessly. Your mind becomes inundated with thoughts of doing, seeing, and having better. You become extremely uncomfortable in your current state of being. Reoccurring frustration and agitation signal that it is time for you to make a change. No matter how much you try to cope, you are not able to find peace. When experiencing a lack of peace and unrest, you realize change is warranted, and vision is calling you. Now is the time to make a move. The hour has come for you to do something different so that you can see and live something different.

Principle 5: "Mind" Your Business: "Boss Up"

It is insanely unrealistic to think that doing the same thing that you have always done would yield anything other than what you have always seen. Have you ever heard, insanity is doing the same thing over and over but expecting different results? Insanity is defined as a severely disordered state of mind, usually occurring as a specific disorder ("Insanity," 2020). It is safe to assume that anyone who practices the same behaviors and expects different outcomes lives in a delusional reality.

So, the question is, "What do you do if you want things to change? How do you change your disordered thinking and mind?" The answer is simple; you must bring order to your thoughts. If you really want to experience a change, you will become obsessed with change. Change can become addictive and consume all your thoughts. The concept of change will follow you everywhere you go and eventually force you to pursue it.

To see change, you must meditate on what you want to see. You must begin to "mind your own business" (your ideas, family, profession, relationships, etc.) Which is to incessantly think and attend to what you want to change and do what you need to do to bring about the changes that you so desire. Albert Einstein said, ***"We cannot solve our problems with the same level of thinking that created them."*** Therefore, you must begin changing your negative thoughts about whatever your "it" is and replace them with positive thoughts about your circumstances. You have to believe that your situation will change and get better. When you become desperate for change, you will wake up and go to sleep with change on your mind, meditate on it throughout the day, and begin to make the necessary steps to see change.

You must also renew your mind and believe that you will see a change. If you want to transform some things in your life, you have got to renew your mind concerning those things and make positive affirmations daily about yourself and your situation. It is also imperative that you glean from others that recognize your worth, encourage and motivate you, and believe in your ability to make the changes you desire.

You must be intentional in transforming every negative thought into a positive one. Have you ever given any thought to what you regularly think about during the day? If not, I urge you to do so. Otherwise, you will continue to contemplate unwanted notions, the worst about your condition, and lose hope that things will ever change. Redirect your ideas on how or what you can do to improve your circumstance. Visualize yourself in a favorable state of being, marriage, home, business, and financial position. Remember what you think about can potentially turn into your reality. If you draw inaccurate conclusions about who you are, what you are capable of, and what you can have, you limit your growth, prosperity, and future potential.

> *"We can not solve our problems with the same level of thinking that created them."*
> *-Albert Einstein*

Mind Over Matter

Your thoughts are a gateway to self-fulfilling prophecies and self-perpetuating cycles. *Your thoughts directly affect your feelings and behaviors.* For example, if you think you will never lose weight, then you will feel like you are not strong or disciplined enough to lose weight. Your actions will reflect your thoughts of never losing weight, which will reinforce your belief that you will never lose weight, and you will not lose weight.

If you believe that you cannot have a successful business, then you will never take the necessary steps to start the business. Your lack

Principle 5: "Mind" Your Business: "Boss Up"

of confidence reinforces your belief that you can never have what you desire to achieve. If you think you will fail at something, your feelings and actions will follow those thoughts, and you will become a product of your thoughts.

Whatever you think about, you start to believe, and that belief ultimately becomes your reality. *When you believe something, you begin to seek evidence that confirms your views.* So why not change your thinking. Start accepting that you can do and have whatever you desire. Then seek evidence that substantiates those beliefs.

Have you ever entertained the idea that it may not be your lack of talents, gifts, or abilities that are hindering your change or forward progression? It just might be your thoughts and beliefs that are keeping you in bondage from moving forth to a better future. For clarity, I am not saying that you can think something and just miraculously have it. I am saying that ***positive thoughts prompt positive actions which enhance your chances for successful outcomes.***

Your beliefs do not define your destiny, but they definitely have the power to alter it. So, modify your beliefs before they manifest. If you want to have better, you must think better and then do better. Mahatma Gandhi said it like this, **"Your beliefs become your words; your words become your actions, your actions become your habits, your habits become your values, and your values become your destiny." The Bible proclaims "For as he thinks in his heart, so is he (Proverbs 23:7 New King James Version)."** Plainly speaking, if you believe that you can do something, your actions will confirm your belief.

In order to change your thoughts, you have to start hearing and believing that you can do something, that you have greatness inside of you, and you can do great things. You must read, speak, and listen to positive messages and affirmations daily concerning you, your life, and future. Your faith increases merely by hearing. I encourage you to confess every day, that:

"I AM GREAT AND I CAN AND WILL DO GREAT THINGS."

"I AM GIFTED AND TALENTED, AND I CAN DO THIS."

"I WILL ACCOMPLISH THIS AND I WILL BE SUCCESSFUL."

You have to confess that:

"MY THOUGHTS ARE CHANGING, AND MY THOUGHTS ARE POSITIVE."

"I WILL FINISH COLLEGE."

"I WILL HAVE MY OWN BUSINESS."

"MY BUSINESS WILL BE SUCCESSFUL."

"MY CHILD WILL TURN HIS/HER LIFE AROUND FOR THE BETTER."

"I WILL NOT BE SINGLE FOR THE REST OF MY LIFE, BUT I WILL MEET THE RIGHT PERSON, AND I WILL GET MARRIED."

"I WILL WRITE THE BOOK."

"I AM HEALED."

"I AM DELIVERED."

"I WILL HAVE A BETTER MARRIAGE AND A BETTER RELATIONSHIP WITH MY CHILDREN."

Principle 5: "Mind" Your Business: "Boss Up"

"MY LIFE IS CHANGING, AND I WILL FULFILL MY VISION AND LIVE MY BEST LIFE!"

> *Your thoughts are a gateway to self-fulfilling prophecies and self-perpetuating cycles.*

Whatever it is that you want, you must confess and believe that it can and will happen. If you believe that things will not change, you will never lose weight, your marriage is over, and your finances will not improve, you can expect those beliefs to turn into your reality. On the other hand, if you believe that you will have positive outcomes, you open yourself to the likelihood you will. You must do whatever it takes to create a positive environment and thinking pattern. If it means posting enlightening declarations in your phone, car, on your mirror, and at work, then do so. When you get desperate enough for change and want to see your vision come to pass, you will get up, step up, and start "minding" your business by accepting that you can have it and accomplish it.

The vastness of the mind is indescribable. ***Its influence can curve your reality to mirror your perspective***. You can influence your situation more by thinking about it strategically, as opposed to arbitrarily reacting to it. ***If you speak and believe that something will happen, you have the power to create a world around you that reflects your expectations.***

The bottom line is, if you want to take charge of your life, you must take control of your thoughts and words and redirect them toward your desired outcome. You must believe that you will see the result you crave. You have to believe in yourself and that something good can happen to you and through you. For example, if you want to have your own business or be a visionary, *then you must think like a BOSS (**Believe in Owning Something**

THE VISION BLUEPRINT

Successful). *You should believe like a BOSS, walk like a BOSS, and make moves like a BOSS)*. You must believe that you will have a successful, sustainable outcome with your vision or business.

Regardless of the area in life that you want to see change, you must take control of it and not allow it to control you. You must BOSS UP! You have to take control of whatever it is in your life that you need to change or conquer. Take control and boss up over your thoughts, relationships, marriage, children, finances, health, vision, and overall well-being. Make no mistake, by no means am I telling you to boss over anyone but yourself. However, I am encouraging you to level up and decide to start initiating changes in areas of your life where you would like to see a difference. I am urging you to:
- → TAKE CONTROL of your thoughts
- → TAKE CONTROL of your beliefs
- → TAKE CONTROL of your actions
- → TAKE CONTROL of your situation
- → TAKE CONTROL of your relationship
- → TAKE CONTROL of your life
- → TAKE CONTROL of your future

Stop letting your past affect your expectations. Yes, it happened, but it is time to dry your eyes, stop living in pity, forgive, boss up, and move forward. You must take back your power. *You will never know the climate of the water or if you can handle the waves if you never get in.* ***It is time for you to BOSS UP. Stop letting your situations control you! If you don't like where you are in life or what is going on in your life, change your mind about it, and then change it***. If you are tired of going to a 9-5 job every day with limited benefits and pay, change it. For example, you have to start to believe that you can be your own boss, that you can set your own pay, vacations, and schedule so that you can take off when you want to without limitations or permission. Start believing that you are just as or more capable as anyone else to do whatever you put your mind to doing. If you BELIEVE that you will succeed,

Principle 5: "Mind" Your Business: "Boss Up"

then you WILL succeed. *A REAL BOSS NEVER gives up, but BOSSES UP!*

Take the Limits Off

You must learn to take the limits off your mind and life. There are no limitations on who you can be or what you can accomplish or what you can have. Your only real limitation is YOU! *A limited mind begets a limited life*. We have all heard the saying, "the sky is the limit." Well, I would have to somewhat disagree with that statement. The reality is that the sky will be your limit if that is what you believe. However, if you believe there is no limit, then not even it can hinder the vastness of the things that you can accomplish. You can function without restrictions once you put your mind to it and aggressively and persistently "mind your business."

It does not matter what your background is or where you come from, where you live, or that you do not have a degree or money, you can still think and change your way out of a hopeless situation. If *you use your mind as the driving force in believing that you can do it, you can change it, you can be it, and you can have it*. You must use your mind, gifts, talents, abilities, and resources to execute your vision. Your mind and thoughts can take you beyond your current situation if you let them. However, **you cannot imprison your thoughts to just the confines of your mind, but you must cultivate them to grow to produce a manifested harvest in your life.**

> *A limited mind begets a limited life.*

THE VISION BLUEPRINT

Mind Wars

I am not saying that it is easy to change years of defeated, negative thoughts overnight. However, they can change with intentional effort and time. It may take time simply because the mind is a battlefield. War takes place in the mind. Psychologists say we have two thought systems: System 1 and System 2 (Kahneman, 2011).

The *System 1 Theory* explains that your automatic, unconscious immediate thoughts and impulses come directly from your body. You have no control over your thoughts (Kahneman, 2011). It is the body's natural response to your circumstances. With this theory, thoughts arise as survival from past experiences, and your brain tries not to overexert itself and optimize energy, so it accepts these thoughts as truth. Your mind grasps and agrees with the initial negative thinking while allowing it to take precedence over positive thinking. Unfortunately, when you allow System 1 to control your thoughts, you have to fight for System 2 to dominate.

System 2 is the conscious dashboard in your mind. It is where you have to exert energy to control your thoughts (Kahneman, 2011). System 2 is where you can directly control, motivate, and form your own thoughts and immediate behaviors without responding as you have in the past.

So, the mind battles between System 1 (unconscious mind) and System 2 (conscious mind). Only when we mature, retrain our thoughts, push past survival thinking to successful thinking, and boss up are we motivated to get up and execute our vision.

> *If you speak and believe that something will happen, you have the power to create a world around you that reflects your expectations.*

Principle 5: "Mind" Your Business: "Boss Up"

Successful people do not just survive; they thrive. Negative thoughts continue to surface because your mind has habitually accepted them, so unconsciously, you think negative thoughts first. If you want success and change in your life, you are going to have to fight for it. Vision execution is not for the weak, timid, or fearful. It requires you to put on your camo, roll up your sleeves, put on your boxing gloves, running shoes and whole armor and fight for your destiny, and not take "no" for an answer. You are going to have to redirect your mind to think positive BOSS thoughts, and eventually, those paralyzing, unproductive thoughts will be dominated by System 2 and deteriorate. Then you will not have to fight to think like a BOSS anymore because your mind will be conditioned to think like a BOSS, act like a BOSS, make moves like a BOSS, and eventually you will become a BOSS!

To mind your business and BOSS up, you must acknowledge where your thoughts are so that you can adjust them to what you want them to be. To successfully execute your vision, you must examine your thoughts by asking yourself some thought-provoking questions.

THE VISION BLUEPRINT

REFLECTIONS

What do you find yourself thinking about throughout your day?

What are your positive thoughts? Write them down and meditate on them daily.

What are your negative thoughts? For every negative thought, I challenge you to write and meditate on a positive thought.

What are you saying about yourself throughout the day?

What are you consistently saying about your life and your future?

Write positive affirmations concerning yourself. Write positive affirmations about your life.

What areas of your life do you need to "Boss Up" and take control of? List some things that you can do to begin to initiate the changes that you want to see.

Principle 5: "Mind" Your Business: "Boss Up"

PRAYER OF INSPIRATION

Lord, please help me to accept that I am someone that you have chosen to make a difference, someone who is special and different. Help me to use my difference to make a difference. Give me the mindset of a leader and a change agent. Make me a mastermind at changing my life and the lives of others. Help me to see myself as a world changer, teacher, mentor, encourager, catalyst, vision executor, and purpose pursuer. Help me to think BIG and know that there are no limits with you, and the plans that you have for me are BIGGER than I can ever imagine. Help me to remember your Word in Ecclesiastes 3:20, that you would do exceedingly, abundantly, above all that I could ask or think according to the power that worketh in us. Help me to understand that nothing is too hard for me to do and that all things are possible with you. Help me to think BIG, SPEAK BIG, ACT BIG, and RECEIVE BIG! Give me the heart of a true visionary and give me a great desire to fulfill the vision that you have given me. Allow others to see you in me and see me as your child and your chosen one. Help them to see that I'm special and favored in Your eyes. Help me to remember and know that I am an heir to you. Help me to remember that you are the King and that I am a part of your Royal Priesthood. Remind me that I am blessed and highly favored, and that I am victorious in all that I say and do because of your Son. Lord, I thank you that whatever I set my hands to do, you said you would bless it, and wherever I tread my feet, you said you would give it to me. Lord, I trust you and the plans you have for me, and I believe in them, and you and I receive them by faith. In Jesus Name, Amen!

PRINCIPLE 6:
PURSUE R & R (RESEARCH & RELATIONSHIPS)

Principle 6: "Pursue R & R (Research & Relationship)

Principle 6:
Pursue R & R (Research & Relationships)

Once you have acknowledged your current reality, discovered yourself, recognized your worth, sized up your circle, and *bossed up*, the next paramount principle to executing your vision is to acquire R&R, no not "*Rest and Relaxation*," not just yet. In this case, R&R is representative of Research & Relationships. Now is the time to do the research and develop pivotal relationships so that you can successfully execute your vision.

The fact that you have reached this chapter is a clear indication that you are inspired to test the water and follow the blueprint. It is time to begin or expand your research on things that you desire to do

THE VISION BLUEPRINT

and seek relationships with those who can accompany you in bringing your vision to fruition. Hopefully, by now, you have assessed your desires, passions, and priorities and have written them down. You are now ready to research and solicit relationships to assist you with getting it done.

So, you might ask, "why do I have to research it when I already have some knowledge about it, and know someone already doing it?" Well, the answer is simple; things are constantly changing, and researching will update, enhance, and expand the knowledge you already have. Research allows you to find out everything that is written about that subject to assist you with perfecting your vision.

Before you execute a vision, it is wise and imperative that you research what you desire to do or want to accomplish. You need to find out the best way to do it, as well as how not to. Find out what is being attempted and accomplished. It is important to examine what others have learned from their successes and failures. Connect with those who are currently doing what you would like to do. You must network with those who are willing to share their knowledge and expertise, contacts, and resources. Researching is vital to your process. It is necessary that you consistently research your vision. Relentlessly, find ways to improve it, stay abreast of current trends as well as wants and needs of those that you desire to serve.

Nancy Shenker, President of the ONswitch, LLC marketing firm, said it best, "Rather than taking time to thoroughly plan and research, they sometimes plow ahead with executing only to spend valuable dollars on unfocused or untargeted activities," (Spaeder, 2020). Research is of the utmost importance when executing any type of service or business. *You need to understand your market before moving forward.* Knowing your market helps you to enhance and perfect your service, which improves your company, products, relations, and profit. You can obtain information for your vision from websites, social media, Google, journals, other

Principle 6: "Pursue R & R (Research & Relationship)

business professionals in the industry, governmental agencies, etc. Research gives you a glimpse of the productivity and sustainability of your vision. It is one thing to have a vision or an idea and another to successfully implement it. It is of the utmost importance to take time to conduct research to perfect and execute your vision. Then form relationships to help devise a plan to explore its' feasibility and profitability.

Knowledge is Power

When conducting your research, there are four things that *Business Daily News mentioned that* you must keep in mind (D'Angelo, 2019).

1) *KNOW YOUR TARGET AUDIENCE*

Your research should focus on the people you plan to target with your business or service. You need to know your customer's likes, dislikes, and needs as it relates to your services. The best way to learn all of this valuable information is by studying your target audience. How do you study them? You examine by surveying and listening. Then structure your service(s) around what you discovered from your research. Listen and take the information you gathered and give them what they need and want.

2) *KNOW YOUR COMPETITION*

You need to know your competitors. Learn their business strategies as if they were your own. Study your competitor's target audience. Study their sales, profit, specific service, etc. See what you can gain from your competition and what you can learn from their successes and failures. Observe their methods to pinpoint gaps in the services they provide. You can model your competitor's concept, but you must find your niche to set you apart. Ask others about your competitors and what they think needs improvement.

THE VISION BLUEPRINT

After you find out what your competition is not doing, capitalize on that information, and give the people the service they desire.

The ultimate goal is to find out what your competition's weaknesses are and use them to your advantage. Then take that knowledge and create a better business or service that meets the needs of your target audience with higher profitability and sustainability.

3) *KNOW CUSTOMER SERVICE*

The saying, "the customer is always right'" is a truth that can make or break your business. I hate to break this to you; unfortunately, in business, the customer *is* indeed always right. You must make it a priority to find out what your customers want and deliver it to them with grace without retaliation. You just may have to lay down your pride and submit to meeting their needs.

Customer competition is inevitable. However, the Accenture 2013 Global Consumer Pulse Survey reported that "Customers choose to patronize businesses where they receive the best customer service versus the best price." Customers return to businesses where they are highly satisfied and receive excellent customer service. Pleased customers tend to become long-standing customers and become mobile advertisements for your business.

In college, I enrolled in an entrepreneurship class. The presenter asks me to interview someone who owned a business. I chose to interview my father, Earl Lee Richardson, Sr., who was a mortician and a funeral home business owner. One of the questions that I asked him was, what do you do for advertising? His response was profound yet puzzling. He responded by saying, "Nothing." I said, what do you mean, nothing? He said, "Baby, if you *treat people with respect, and care, and provide them with the best service possible, they will do the advertising for you.*" I learned that your service is your best commercial or billboard. Customers

Principle 6: "Pursue R & R (Research & Relationship)

can generate a snowball effect of advertisement for your business. By treating others with respect and care, my father lived up to his business motto of "We provide more than service, we care."

Another critical nugget is never *promise your customers something that you cannot deliver*. My father and his siblings were able to sustain the success of my grandparents, Alexander and Melissa Richardson's legacy of Richardson Funeral Home, Inc. for over 55 years because they put the needs and wants of their customers first. There are countless stories from repeat, satisfied customers of Richardson's Funeral Home. These families spoke of the caring heart and compassion that my father demonstrated during their time of need and not to mention the multiple compliments about the exceptional service they received. Thanks to his consistent concern and care for his customers, we are blessed to have faithful, loyal customers for years to come.

Repeat customers usually return because they are satisfied, appreciated, and recognized. An example of this is people supporting a church by membership. Pastors and church leaders must form relationships and recognize the gifts, abilities, and talents existing within the membership. The church will only experience growth when executing excellence, great leadership, structure, and order. For example, church services should start promptly on time, and all leaders should be in position. On any given Sunday, the choir must be present and sing faithfully and passionately. The ushers, greeters, deacons, and church mothers should all serve with a smile, love, and compassion. The media ministry must be in place to ensure the sound is in order. The parking lot attendants are there to direct traffic to make parking easy for attendees. The ministers and elders are in place to pray and serve the people. The youth leaders are in stations to accept and teach the children. The pastoral care team is there to assist the pastor. The evangelism team faithfully participates in ministry outreach and leading others to Christ. The church administrative team is there to oversee church operations effectively.

THE VISION BLUEPRINT

In addition to training others to serve with excellence and pastoring a multitude of people, it is imperative that the pastor visit and pray with members. The church success depends on the pastor leading, helping, and caring for members. The members feel special knowing that they have a pastor they can relate to and knows who they are. People want a pastor that shows compassion and love towards them, which causes them to come back time and time again. This type of service exemplifies that *satisfied people receiving consistent, excellent service can potentially become lifetime consumers.* Remember, commitment and connection with those you serve predicate continued support and growth. You must consistently connect, communicate with them, and listen to them to meet their needs and serve them effectively.

> ***Never promise your customers something that you can't deliver.***

According to the CEO of the Urban ladder, a satisfied customer will contribute up to 2.6 times more revenue as compared to an unsatisfied customer (Arogyalokesh, 2020). Consistency in the provision of service contributes to continued revenue from satisfied customers. The White House Office of Consumer Affairs reported that 13 percent of clients usually tell up to 20 people about their customer experiences. These actions demonstrate that unsatisfied customers can also negatively impact your business tremendously. You must understand the detrimental impact unfavorable customer relations can have on your business or service. It is imperative that you routinely monitor and improve customer relations to maintain and increase your customers and revenue. Prioritizing *customer satisfaction, coupled with establishing and maintaining high customer relations, produces continued customer support and business productivity and profit.*

Principle 6: "Pursue R & R (Research & Relationship)

Terrific customer service is what separates good businesses from great businesses. It distinguishes the four or five-star companies from two or three-star companies. Good customer service is what puts you on top of your competitors. It is not just about appropriately greeting and servicing your customers, but also about managing every aspect of your business with your customers in mind. Providing adequate service includes personal meetings, telephone interactions, social media engagements, quick and efficient service responses, providing product and service information, continuing education and product development, immediately handling customer concerns and complaints, and managing overall customer relations.

4) *KNOW YOUR CLIMATE*

It is not enough to execute your vision; you also must know where the execution should take place. Knowing your climate means knowing your atmosphere. *Location is vital to the success of your vision or business*. Know your audience and their location. Where do you plan to offer your services? Today, physical stores are gradually fading away. Many brick and mortar businesses are going out of business or have transitioned to offer online services. So, the question is, where can you find your target audience? If you are targeting young adults, they tend to spend a massive amount of time on social media, so that may be a suitable place to launch or advertise a business. Today's life-changing events have forced everyone to embrace a new normal of accessing products and business services online. So, now just may be the time to start or share your vision online.

Since this generation is concerned with convenience, you may also need to consider having a mobile business where you go to your customers to provide your service. On the other hand, older adults may spend more time in physical stores. So, discover your target audience and position your business location around them. ***Your location should never be an inconvenience to your customers***.

THE VISION BLUEPRINT

The more convenient your business/service is to your audience, the more successful your business is likely to be. *Your location should always be customer-centered.*

Other important things to consider when executing your vision, starting a business, or providing a service:

- *Seek legal counsel to find out the advantages and disadvantages of providing a service or starting a business.* Protective and preventive legal coverage and preparation are imperative for business sustainability and success. Find a lawyer that specializes in business law to direct you on:
    o Applying for a business license
    o Obtaining your articles of incorporation,
    o Establishing an employee identification number
    o Acquiring business and personal liability insurance
  Legal assistance will give you security in knowing that you are following appropriate and best business practices that are feasible and profitable.

- *Know the right timing to execute your vision.* You must study the economy and the needs of society to gage when it is lucrative and conducive to offer a particular service or start a business. Also, identify pitfalls that can make or break your business upon execution. Recognize that expansion of services should not take place until the timing is right. For example, due to the current climate of our nation, it's a great time to provide online services.

- *Seek resources and capital.* First, start with using what you have in your hand. What do you already possess that can assist you in executing your vision? Secondly, who do you have around you to aid with your vision (i.e., friends, family, business relationships)? Lastly, seek out business loans or grants from the Small Business Association, financial institutions, corporations, and other resources.

Principle 6: "Pursue R & R (Research & Relationship)

You also need to seek professional assistance from accounting professionals concerning payroll, federal and state taxes, and revenue management, etc.

- *Know the risk.* Before executing your vision, know your risks. Know the industry that you are embarking upon by researching it thoroughly. You should not go into any area of interest without knowing everything there is about the area. Be prepared for risks, always have a backup plan, and cover yourself with the proper insurances.

RELATIONSHIPS

Vision-ships

Relationships are critical when executing your vision. *You don't just need relationships, but you need "vision-ships."* These are relationships with people that are interested and supportive in assisting you with executing your vision. In addition to having the right people in your intimate circle, you should also encompass yourself with those who are successful in doing what you are trying to accomplish. Surround yourself with those who know the service/business that you desire to provide. You also need mentors who have the desire to assist you and want to see you succeed. **Vision-ships should be willing, purposeful, and impactful.**

Strive to connect yourself with those willing to invest time and resources that contribute to your success. Spend time with people who have successfully implemented their vision and demonstrated productivity. Mentors should be easily accessible and willing to go the extra mile to see you succeed. Your mentor should be a teacher and encourager. Always remember that every person you encounter in your scope of interest or expertise is a prospective mentor or resource. Therefore, it behooves you to treat those you encounter with integrity and respect.

THE VISION BLUEPRINT

> *Visionships should be willing, purposeful and impactful.*

You should embrace those who are willing to assist you with bringing your vision to pass. Executing your vision will not only take encouragement but a lot of time and effort. *You need people around you that believe in your vision so much that they are willing to get in the water with you. I am speaking of people who will put in the time and effort to help you execute or enhance it.* You need those who will help you research the business, connect you with the right resources, and help you take care of the logistics and practicalities.

Business-Client Relationships

Relationships have the potential to make or break your vision. *Clients are looking for a product, business, or service that they can trust.* They are looking for a business or person that displays consistency in their product or services. If you want to gain the trust of your clients, you need to be dependable and reliable. Your clients need to know that they can expect to receive exceptional services and or products from you every time. They want to feel secure in knowing that if you fall short, you are willing to correct your fault or compensate them for your mishap immediately. *Clients need to know that you appreciate their business and continued support.* You can show them by giving back to them via discounts, free services, and by hosting and inviting them to customer appreciation events. Building and sustaining client-business relationships are vital to creating a successful business or service.

Principle 6: "Pursue R & R (Research & Relationship)

Business-Employee Relationships

Your employees are a direct connection to your customers and the overall success of your business. Form good business-employee relationships and remember that it is your employees that promote or sell your products and services. They need to know that you are interested in what concerns them. You must reassure them that they are not just a number to you, but that you appreciate them and that they are an asset to the team. Make a point to let them know that what concerns them, concerns you.

Employees are encouraged when their voices and concerns receive attention. They experience boosts in morale when employers are genuinely concerned about them, which enhances business-employee relations, productivity, and revenue. Most employees are not just interested in getting more money, but they are interested in being respected, valued, and appreciated. Many employers experience a high turnover rate because employees feel devalued, disrespected, and unappreciated; therefore, resignation is an easy decision. If you want to maintain good employees, it is your job to give them a reason to continue working with you. You must make them feel like they are vested in your company and play an integral part in all successes.

It is important to have satisfied employees who want to promote and enhance your business. *Happy employees become business advertisement resources.* On the other hand, unhappy employees can become negative advertisements mirroring unhappy customers, ultimately leading to adverse business outcomes. Appreciate your employees by remaining visible and accessible to them, acknowledging and complimenting their performance, offering incentives, and giving bonuses.

If you want your business to be successful, then you must develop good business-customer and employee relationships.

THE VISION BLUEPRINT

7 Ways to Improve Client and Employee Relationships:

1. Provide regular training on customer services and compassion, company policies, procedures, and products.
2. Create a professional and comfortable working atmosphere for employees to boost employee morale and satisfaction.
3. Establish an excellent and efficient client grievance protocol.
4. Display integrity and loyalty to employees and customers.
5. Be accessible, relatable, and compassionate toward customers and employees.
6. Establish an advisory board and quality team for business improvement.
7. Provide ongoing instruction on having a 5-star mentality and treating consumers with the utmost care and respect.

Ask yourself, what would make you patronize a business time and time again. What would make you buy products over and over? Use those same reasons to find your niche, conduct your research, and seek out relationships. Allow it to assist you with developing your vision, business, product, or service that is successful and viable.

To successfully execute your vision, ask yourself some vital questions to ensure that you have conducted the proper research, and formed the right relationships or vision-ships.

Principle 6: "Pursue R & R (Research & Relationship)

REFLECTIONS

What are the major components of your vision/business plan?

Who are other businesses or people who have a similar vision or offer comparable services?

Who have you chosen as a mentor(s)?

What research have you found to be beneficial to your business/vision?

What research do you still have left to do?

What area is lacking with those businesses or persons who offer similar services/products?

What do you plan to do to separate your vision/business from the rest?

How do you plan to retain customers and improve customer satisfaction?

How do you plan to retain employees and improve employee satisfaction?

What viable relationships or vision-ships do you currently have or would like to have?

THE VISION BLUEPRINT

PRAYER OF INSPIRATION

Lord, I thank you for your help with giving me the wisdom to execute the vision and purpose you have given me. Please give me divine grace and favor to connect with people who will help me bring my vision to pass. Send a willing mentor in my life to help me with bringing my vision to fruition. Help me to develop meaningful, productive, real relationships needed to help and assist me wherever needed. Lord, lead and direct me by your Spirit from start to finish. Give me the wisdom, knowledge, and understanding required to fulfill the vision. Help me to write it out, lift it off the pages, and execute the vision. Lord, as I do my part, I ask that you guide me and walk with me every step of the way. Speak to my heart and let me know whether to turn left or right or to be still until you say move. Please bring clarity to the confusion of what I should be doing. Help me to recognize real people and develop purpose-driven, divinely appointed relationships. Allow your Spirit to teach me all that I need to know about my vision and help me to do all that I need to do to bring it to pass. Give me a solid, sustainable, successful vision and execution plan. Help me to implement it with ease. Give me divine grace and favor with everyone that I encounter. Let them see your purpose and plan when I present my vision to them. Touch hearts to help me bring it to pass for your glory and the good of your people. Lord, help me to be the best employer and visionary that I can be. Please send faithful people and clients in my life. Let them come from the north, south, east, and west. I promise when it's all said and done, I will give you all the glory, honor, and praise for what you have done. Most importantly, give me the wisdom and people in my life to help me so that I can help others. Lord, I love you, thank you, and I trust you to bring it to pass. In Jesus' name, I pray, Amen.

PRINCIPLE 7: "WORK" IT

Principle 7: "Work" It

One vital principle of this process is strategizing a plan and working to execute your vision. Planning proceeds the work. It is one thing to have an idea in your mind and to put it on paper, but it is another thing to take it off the paper and put your words into action. One valuable thing that Pastor Eric A. Williams stated is that *"Between the want and the wait is the WORK."* To see your vision come to pass, you have to work it. A vision does not just happen by osmosis. It materializes when you put in the work to bring it to fruition.

Typically, attempting something new can stimulate fear. You must push past your fears and initiate your plan. FEAR is known to be an acronym for (*False Evidence Appearing Real*). Fear of failure will hinder you from planning your work and working your plan. It can paralyze you and trigger unproductivity. Fear will potentially prompt your mind to magnify and meditate on everything that could go wrong while attempting to turn your vision into reality.

Principle 7: "Work" It

Fear is an enemy to Vision. So, to push past fears, you must do what **Joyce Meyers said, "*Do it Afraid!*"** You must face your fears head-on by doing it anyway. Think about it; you are already afraid to stay in the current state that you are in, so why not get up, act, and fulfill your vision. It is okay to be scared, but it is not okay for you to allow fear to hinder you from progressing in life. It's time to take back your power from fear and get to work in the face of it.

"With vision, there is no room to be frightened. No reason for intimidation. It's time to march forward! Let's be confident and positive!"

- Charles Swindoll

To do this, you must dispel fear. You must be motivated and encouraged to believe that YOUR vision can come to pass. One way to move from fear to faith is by listening to motivational messages from other visionaries and by writing and speaking inspirational "I-messages."

What are "I-messages," you ask? Well, "I-messages" are your "personal" messages, confessions, and aspirations.

Here are some examples of "I-messages." You must begin to believe and speak:

"I can do this by the strength, wisdom, and grace of God!"

"I am worthy, and I love me, unconditionally!"

"I can do all things through Christ that strengthens me!"

"I will execute my vision, and it will be successful!"

"I will work faithfully and persistently to fulfill my vision!"

"I will overcome my feelings and obstacles and not stop until my vision manifests!"

"I have everything I need internally and externally to accomplish this!"

"I believe if God did it for others, He can and will do it for me!

"I will have what God says that I can have by this time next year!"

"I WIN, and I am Victorious!"

> *Fear is an enemy to Vision.*

I strongly encourage you to profess these things daily or take some time to develop your own "I-messages." Affirming these things does not miraculously bring your vision to pass but speaking these things can motivate you to get up and **"work it to pass."** Know that your vision will work if you work it! However, to work, you must plan out what you need to do and start to walk and work out those plans daily.

Write the Vision

The bible says **"Write the vision, and inscribe it on tablets, that the one who reads it may run. For the vision is yet for the appointed time; it hastens toward the goal, and it will not fail. Though it tarries, wait for it; for it will certainly come, it will not delay (Habakkuk 2:2-3 New King James Version)."** Simply put, writing your vision helps to motivate and encourage you to remember and work your vision, and eventually, you will see your

Principle 7: "Work" It

vision. Writing out a vision or business plan helps you to see things clearly, and it gives you more direction. It gives you a strategy for executing your vision. It helps you to walk out your

> *"Write the vision, and inscribe it on tablets, that the one who reads it may run. For the vision is yet for the appointed time; it hastens toward the goal and it will not fail. Though it tarries, wait for it; for it will certainly come, it will not delay."*

vision one step and one day at a time.

Writing the vision down helps you not to forget and doubt it when things are happening in your life that are contrary to your vision. Consistently writing and reading your vision motivates and encourages you. Repeating it forces it to take root in your heart and prompts you to believe in and act on it.

As you take small steps to fulfill your vision, you become more and more encouraged and inspired to execute it. You may start off walking your vision out, but the more you walk it out and see it coming to fruition, it will cause you to start running it out. It will make you want to work harder and harder to bring it to pass. Things will become more apparent as you begin taking steps to execute your vision. *As you work, things will start to connect, and answers will be revealed to intimidating questions concerning your vision. Your direction will begin to become more defined.*

Writing your business or vision plan is pivotal when executing your vision. It is necessary to direct you and to impress potential supporters and investors. Your written plan should be concise, yet compelling, and display passion.

THE VISION BLUEPRINT

The Small Business Administration suggests that your business plan includes the following:
- ➢ Explanation of the products and services that you will provide.
- ➢ Summary of your business vision.
- ➢ Lists statistics and research on your business.
- ➢ Defines your:
  - o Business management and organization structure
  - o Advertising strategies
  - o Funding and financial projections
  - o Personal qualifications

As previously mentioned, when writing your plan, it is vital to do your research first to obtain everything you need to know about your idea. Research helps determine what services to offer, who to serve, how those services will profit, and how to make your service unique.

Marketing your vision/business is a must. You must have an exceptional marketing strategy. It is recommended that you use every opportunity for advertising (i.e., social media platforms, public speaking engagements, people, etc.). If you are starting a new business, you will benefit from hiring a marketing and branding specialist. The specialist will help to create an aggressive marketing strategy, build your brand, and increase the success of your business. You will also need to develop a marketing plan that speaks to potential clients and investors.

The focal component of your business plan is to explain the what and why of your proposal. It gives insight as it relates to your interest and motivation for desiring it. The goal is that the reviewer is seduced by the passion and purpose of your plan. *You want to capture the reader's heart with the intent of your passion because the profit has not come yet.* When your supporters and investors are captivated by your zeal, they will be comforted in knowing that you are not just doing it for monetary gain. *Your passion helps*

Principle 7: "Work" It

solidify your vision commitment with them and increases the probability they will support and fund your vision.

It's Time to Move

Recently, one of my deceased father's loyal customers came to patronize the business and informed us that she had a dream about him. She said in the dream he told her, "it was time to move." What he said to her did not resonate with her. She did not realize that she was led there to confirm this word to me. That confirmed word was not just for me, but it was for me to share with YOU.

It is time for you to move and work your business/vision plan and overcome excuses and procrastination. It is time for you to "get up, boss up, and go up." You can no longer just dream about it or talk about it, but it is time for you to be about it." It is time for you to get up and move and make things happen. It is time to **"Put your work where your mouth is!"**

To begin executing your vision, you need to see your vision clearly. **You must SEE it before you can SEE it!** Imagine it in your mind before you see it manifested in the natural. **Vision is defined as the ability to think about or plan the future with imagination or wisdom ("Vision," 2020)."** Vision gives you hope and inspiration. George Barna stated, **"*vision is a clear mental image of a preferable future imparted by God to His chosen servants and is based upon an accurate understanding of God, self, and circumstances."*** Vision gives you the ability to see when there is no understanding. Vision permits you to see what others who have eyes cannot see. It sees no limitations and penetrates all barriers. It is a picture that comes from your spirit that permeates into your heart and mind. Vision allows your spirit to lead you to where your mind cannot take you.

Having a vision suggests that you are a visionary. **Visionary is defined as one having unusual foresight or imagination ("Visionary," 2020).** *A visionary naturalizes what he/she sees in* *his/her mind*. We all have been created for a purpose and given a vision or purpose to fulfill. The difference between having a vision and being a visionary is visionaries not only see it in their mind, but they also do the work to bring it to pass.

Most people have a vision, but not everyone is a visionary. The only thing that differentiates the vision from the visionary is the WORK!

> ***You must SEE it before you can SEE it!***

Busyness Versus Productivity

One thing that keeps you from working your plan is busyness. I once told someone that I was busy, and they asked me, *"Are you just busy, or are you being productive?"* That question changed my life. It made me start evaluating what I was doing and where I was spending my time. It made me start asking myself if what I was doing was directing me towards fulfilling my vision and doing the things that I was purposed to do. So, I want to ask you the same question. *"Are you busy doing things that are not directing you toward fulfilling your vision? Are you truly being productive and accomplishing things that are helping you work out your vision and purpose?* Whatever you may be doing that is not leading you toward what God purposed you to do or what is in your heart, it is imperative that you redirect your actions toward your purpose.

You can no longer allow anything or anyone to hinder the work of your vision. Other people's agendas and plans for you can easily take you off your vision track. You must recognize these diversions. What others are asking you to do may be useful and helpful, but it still may not be what your heart is leading you to do. It may not be purposeful. Therefore, you must use discernment and

Principle 7: "Work" It

use this vision blueprint to help you continue onto "Vision Highway." *It is okay to help others to accomplish their vision and work. However, you can never get so caught up in helping others fulfill their vision that you never fulfill your own.*

When you have a written plan, it helps you to stay focused, and it serves as your GPS to executing your vision. The early stages of executing your vision are critical. When working out your vision, you should set aside time daily to do something that catapults you to accomplish it. Just think about how many hours you spend on social media, watching television, playing games, or on the telephone, achieving nothing. I challenge you to begin to convert those hours to vision time. You will slowly start seeing your vision come together and eventually come to pass. Use that time to work out the steps in your plan to fulfill your vision. Those steps may entail thinking and writing, making phone calls, setting up and going to meetings, doing research, forming relationships, or encouraging yourself.

Just Say "NO"

One word that will become incredibly significant on your vision journey is the word, "NO." If you are like me, someone who loves to serve and help others, this word is often difficult to exercise. However, when you become overwhelmed and desperate to accomplish those things that are in your heart, you will find yourself using this word more frequently. **You must learn to say "No" to things that may be good things but not vision things.** You will begin to realize that some of the good things that you used to do, have now become distractions and hindrances from what you want and need. Now is the time for you to make tough decisions and say "No" to what you use to do and what others always counted on and expected of you. I must warn you, initially, you will feel uncomfortable with saying "NO." You will experience some animosity and backlash from some of those whom you offer these "NO's." Learn to push past these emotions and just say, "NO!" **You will eventually accept that you are not**

THE VISION BLUEPRINT

necessarily saying "NO" to helping others, but that you are just saying "YES" to your vision. Your response should be that you are not going to be able to assist them because *you have an appointment with destiny that can no longer be rescheduled.* Eventually, people will begin to respect your "NO" even if they don't understand it.

You are probably wondering when you should say, "NO?" Well, you should say "NO" to anything that is detouring you from "Vision Highway." Because *if you continue to detour onto "Distraction Road" and "Nowhere Avenue," you will never make it to "Vision Destination Boulevard."* You must learn to be comfortable with saying "NO" and realize that it is not a bad word. *You should look at it as a necessary, purposeful word. Instead of looking at it negatively, think of "NO" as the acronym for "**New Opportunities**." If you keep saying "yes" to doing visionless things, you will never take advantage of the New Opportunities in front of you*! The word "NO" will help to keep you on the right road to destiny, so I dare you to practice it now and to write down the things that deserve a "NO."

> *You have an appointment with destiny that can no longer be rescheduled.*

Principle 7: "Work" It

There are seven key things that you must consider when working out your vision plan:

1) POSITION FOR VISION

You must position yourself for your vision. Distractions can cloud your vision and cause you to be confused. Imagine how out of focus you can become when pulled in several directions and asked to accomplish a million things. Circumstances such as these are why you must remove yourself from distractions (people and things) and the busyness of life. It is necessary to find a quiet place and position yourself for vision. You must pray and meditate to figure out what your next steps are to fulfill your vision. *You cannot work your plan if you are unsure what your plan is.* Once it becomes clear, it is easier to accomplish what is needed to fulfill your vision. *Vision execution is like a puzzle; once you connect one piece, it becomes easier to figure out the next connecting part.* If you never connect the first piece, you will remain puzzled and paralyzed.

2) PLACE OF VISION

Find the place where your vision becomes clear. When planning your vision, your current place is extremely important. Being in the wrong place can impair you from planning your vision. Being stuck at a visionless job all day for several days a week can hinder you from focusing on planning your vision. You are in the wrong place when you work only to receive a paycheck, and you feel no sense of purpose or self-fulfillment. You experience frustration with jobs and places not directly connected to your destiny because they keep you from executing your vision. In situations like this, you will have to make the necessary time and find a place to begin planning your vision.

Being at home all day taking care of everyone and everything but yourself can also hinder you from planning and working your vision. Your home and workplace can be busy and distracting.

THE VISION BLUEPRINT

Therefore, you will need to find peaceful, quiet places in and outside of the house that will allow you time to plan and work your vision. If you do not position yourself to hear, plan, and work your vision, it may never manifest.

In some instances, you may have to step out on faith and leave your job to fulfill your vision. In others, *God will use clueless pawns on the job to frustrate or terminate you so that you can pursue your vision.* Do not be alarmed or distracted because this is just God pushing you out of prison and into purpose. *God will use your Pharaohs to push you into your promised land*, but Lord have mercy on your Pharaohs. Just thought I would throw that in there! God will do whatever He needs to do and use whomever He needs to use to get you in the place where he wants and needs you to be. Learn to accept what God allows and know that He is working all things together for you to be in the right place at the right time on purpose for a purpose.

3) PURPOSE FOR YOUR VISION

Every real vision has a purpose. You can identify your vision, not just as being something, you want to do, but also something that you know that you were created to do. We all have a vision, yet we all have a different purpose and assignment. ***Vision is never really about you, but always about helping others***. It is about making a difference in the lives of others. I knew I had to write this book to help someone else execute their vision. More often than not, your vision and purpose will be confirmed to you. If it is something that you think you want to do or feel like doing, that feeling may waiver back and forth, so you will probably be less likely to take steps to make it happen. When you experience a true vision, that vision will stay in the forefront of your mind and be embedded in your heart. It will consistently remain the focus of your dreams or fantasies. It is repeatedly confirmed, and it tends to dominate your thoughts.

Principle 7: "Work" It

A real vision never leaves you, it only lies dormant, and it resurrects itself in your heart and mind time after time. Unfortunately, most times we are consumed with pursuing prosperity instead of purpose, and we get detoured from our vision. We have it backwards. We must understand that prosperity is connected to our vision. **You must stop chasing prosperity and chase purpose and prosperity will come.** When you finally realize that purpose and prosperity are attached to your vision; you will be more determined to execute it.

> *Vision is never really about you, but it's always about helping others.*

4) PROTECT YOUR VISION

It is important to protect your vision. Your vision belongs to you, and you cannot assume that everyone will be excited for you or eager to help you fulfill it. Be careful not to share your vision with those that you do not trust because someone else may try to rob or duplicate the idea or talk you out of it. It is critical that you protect your vision until you are ready to execute or enhance it. If you have a vision name or idea, register your name or copyright your idea immediately before anyone can rob you of it. You need to guard your ideas, plans, and niche as if it were top secret, and you were the CIA. You need to secure your vision plans and not disclose them to anyone who is not trustworthy or directly related to assisting you with executing your vision.

5) PREPARE FOR VISION

You are probably wondering what I mean when I say prepare for vision. Well, there is preparation for vision execution. You spiritually prepare your mind and heart and naturally prepare by gathering information, establishing relationships, and writing your vision and plan. You must plan for the "what ifs" when executing your vision. You must ask yourself, "what if this happens in the process," and then come up with potential solutions. However, you must also prepare for post vision execution. Because once you have implemented your vision, you must be ready to maintain the vision and handle overflow and success. Having faith that you can plan and execute your vision prepares you to handle the failures and successes of the process. Make no mistake, vision execution is time consuming. It is not a quick, easy process, and it will take several hours a day, months, and maybe even years of planning and working to manifest. So be prepared to be resilient and faithful and vow not to quit until you see it come to fruition.

6) PROCESS YOUR VISION

There is a process in bringing your vision to pass. Process is defined as a series of actions or steps taken in order to achieve an end ("Process," 2020). You must process in your mind where you are and the steps that you need to take to bring it to full manifestation. ***You must process it in your head before you can process it in your life.*** You have to go through your process and know that whatever you have gone through in life was necessary to perfect and equip you to walk in and work out your vision. Process is also equivalent to time, and you must understand that it will not manifest overnight. Know that you will encounter some potholes, crooked roads, detours, hills, mountains, valleys, and dead ends on the road to Vision Destination Boulevard. You must continue to follow the blueprint. Every obstacle, challenge, and situation good or bad are all a part of the process to prepare you for planning, implementing, executing, and sustaining your vision. Nothing in your life "just happened." All you are going through and have gone through has equipped you to execute your vision and walk into your purpose and destiny.

Principle 7: "Work" It

7) PROMOTE YOUR VISION

Promoting or advertising your vision may be the most challenging step. If you are like me, you try to avoid being in the spotlight and the center of attention. You would much rather stay behind the scenes. Well, sorry to disturb you, but vision always brings illumination to people and things. What good is it to execute your vision but never share it with anyone? Remember, **visionaries share their vision with the intent of impacting the lives of others**. To share your vision, you will have to disclose it to others, advertise, and communicate on all public/private media outlets and platforms. Solicit assistance with sharing your vision by employing someone to help promote who you are and what you have to offer. As I struggled with this, God said to me, "You must be unselfish enough to reveal your vision and do what is needed to impact someone else's life." **Ultimately, sharing your vision is not about promoting you, but it's all about helping someone else**.
Promoting your vision is letting others know that you are someone that has something to share that can hopefully assist them with living a better life.

Even though there are many steps to completing your vision, if you never take the first step, it will never manifest. *It is comfortable staying on the shore and playing it safe and never taking a risk to see if you can survive the waves and the climate of the water. Unfortunately, that will eventually cause you to miss opportunities and deprive you of living your best life.* You are wondering, "what if I step in the water and sink?" Well, you should be asking, "what if I step in and swim?" You must have a positive, victorious mindset. You must believe that you can make it. If you do not believe in yourself, then who else will? *Vision not only takes time to manifest, but it will take much faith and persistence in the process.* **Faith is walking out your vision without immediately seeing the full result.** It is like a pregnant woman who is told that she will have a baby in approximately nine months. She must have faith to believe that she will see her baby in nine months, even though she can't naturally see her baby's eyes, bones, vessels, or heart forming. She must have faith enough to believe that what she believes will manifest in a few months. In the meantime, she works to nurture her baby until he/she arrives. *Grab hold to the same kind of faith. Believe that your vision will manifest and continue feeding it even though you do not see results immediately.*

Understand that your success is not mandated upon someone else's approval. All you have to do is believe in yourself and do the work. *Every successful vision started as a seed, but when the seed marries work, it produces the baby, vision, dream, and harvest.* You have waited, thought about, and hoped for it long enough. It is time to stop waiting and dreaming and get up and get off the shore and step in the water, follow the blueprint, do the work, and see the results. **Faith without works is dead (James 2:26 New King James Version).** It is time to resurrect your dream, work it and reap the benefits. Stop being a hindrance to yourself. If you must, put on your life jacket before you step into the water, but decide to step in today. The water may get rough, but you have to be determined to keep swimming and not give up until you have reached your desired destination.

Writing this book was a part of my vision. I finally realized that procrastination and doubt were not getting me anywhere. Therefore, I decided to begin writing a few pages a day during my demanding schedule. What I envisioned and worked for has finally manifested. I decided to get off the shore, step in the water, and follow the blueprint. I am motivated to continue working toward everything that I saw for my life. If I started my vision journey, so can you. So, I dare you to get up and execute your vision.

> *Faith is walking out your vision without immediately seeing the full result.*

Principle 7: "Work" It

REFLECTIONS

What are you afraid of? What's holding you back from executing your vision?

List some of your own personal "I-Messages."

Write out your vision and the necessary steps to get there.

What are some things that are keeping you busy from executing your vision?

What are some productive things that you are doing that are assisting you with manifesting your vision?

Who and what do you need to say "NO" to?

What do you need to do to position yourself for vision?

Where is your place for vision? If you don't have one, find one.

What is the purpose of your vision?

What are you doing to protect your vision?

How will you prepare for your vision?

List the process for fulfilling your vision.

How will you promote your vision?

THE VISION BLUEPRINT

PRAYER OF INSPIRATION

Lord, I thank you for allowing me to make it to the working phase of my vision. I ask that you complete the perfect work that you started in me. I ask you, who is the author and finisher of my faith, to help me to stay faithful and persistent until I see my vision manifested. I ask you to bless everything that I set my hand to do and that you order my every step. I ask that you strategically give me each step to take and instruct me every step of the way. I ask that you allow your spirit to lead, guide, and direct me. Lord, show me which way to turn. Lead me in the path of those that you have designated to assist me with fulfilling my vision. Lead me into the lives of those that you have assigned me to touch. Give me divine grace and favor with everyone connected with bringing my vision to pass. Whenever I get weary, please give me strength to keep going because your strength is perfect in my weakness. Please give me provision for the vision that you have given me. When I don't know what to do next, show me. When I don't understand, explain. When my faith gets weak, increase it. When I feel like giving up, help me not to quit and remind me that quitting is not an option. Lord, I ask that you remove all my fears and replace them with faith. Lord, I pray that you would silence my enemies and every negative voice of the enemy. I ask you to fight every battle of opposition that I face. I thank you that every plot of my enemies against me will not work, and what my enemies meant for evil, you will turn it around for my good. I ask that you remove every obstacle and hindrance that tries to stop me from executing the vision that you have given me. I ask that as I take a step, you will be right there with me holding my hand and walking and talking with me. I thank you that nothing or no one can stop me with you on my side. I thank you for your love and for gracing me with vision. Thank you for choosing me to be a visionary. Lord, I'm off the shore and in the water now, and I need you to keep me above

Principle 7: "Work" It

the water and help me swim to destiny. Lord, I trust and believe that you will. I promise to give you all the glory, honor, and praise during the process and when I reach my destination. In Jesus' name, Amen.

PRINCIPLE 8:
DON'T GIVE UP

Principle 8: Don't Give Up

Visionaries see things, act, and don't stop until they live in what they saw. Visionaries act because they genuinely believe that they can obtain what they see. Their faith is demonstrated by their action. Faith is powerful! It is the fuel needed to execute your vision. There is just something about the influence of faith. Faith will make you do things that you never thought you could do. It enables you to accomplish what seems impossible and unattainable. Faith will make you see when your eyes are closed; move when you don't feel like moving; study when you don't feel like studying; run when you don't even feel like walking, and write when you don't feel like writing. Ask me, I know from experience that faith and belief are unstoppable forces! The Bible defines faith as the substance of things hoped for, the evidence of things not seen (Hebrews 11:1 New King James Version). Faith helps you hold on to hope even when your vision looks as if it will never come to pass. It endows you to believe in what can be, even though you cannot see it tangibly. **Faith gives you X-ray vision**. It provides you with supernatural insight to see through and past every obstacle and circumstance that may be hindering you from executing your vision. Faith is a prerequisite to not giving up.

You must know that anything worth having will not typically come easy. There are going to be times when you get tired, fail, hear "no," get weak, and want to give up, but you have to believe and confess that "***Quitting is NOT an option***." Many people struggle with quitting when they experience failure or when achieving their goals calls for profound work and sacrifice, but you must remember that delay does not mean denial.

Think of what could have happened if Michael Jordan gave up when he consistently missed basketball shots. What may have happened if Steve Jobs stopped trying to perfect the Apple computer? What might have happened if the physician told your parents they would never have a child, and they quit trying? Think of what would have happened if you stayed in school and kept studying?

If you had not quit and accepted no for an answer, where you might be now? Where would Oprah Winfrey and Tyler Perry be if they quit after being denied over and over again? Where would the world be if Martin Luther King, Jr. decided to give up? Several lives, including theirs, would have been immensely impacted if they had given up. Much in the same way, your life and the lives of others that you are assigned to will be affected if you give up.

You can't give up. Someone is depending on you to execute your vision. Your giving up just might cause someone else to give up too. ***There are no benefits to giving up. Giving up hinders your progression, makes you doubt your ability, weakens your faith and distracts and detours you from productivity and success***. Just

Principle 8: Don't Give Up

think if you kept going and did not quit, how much closer would you be to having or doing what you desire.

> **Faith gives you X-ray vision.**

Work Until you See It

Faith does not work alone. Its partner is persistence. It is one thing to believe that you can do something, but it is another thing to keep striving until you conquer and accomplish it. You have to keep believing that you can do it and have it. Your faith will keep you working until you see the manifestation of it. It does not matter who may not believe in you or your vision because it is not their vision; it is yours. Some may have tunnel vision when it comes to your vision, but when your vision is God-given, you will see it clearly. He will give you the ability to see what others cannot see. However, God is so awesome that He will give someone a glimpse of what He has shown you so that they can encourage you or assist you with bringing it to pass. So, NEVER give up on your vision if others may not see what you see. Others seeing it has no bearing on it coming to pass. Always remember that the only thing that really matters is that YOU see it!

Do not let anyone change your vision. People will try to change your vision to fit their vision for your life, but your job is to remember what God showed you. *Do not get distracted and detoured by someone else's vision.* **Do not taint your vision by looking through someone else's lens. Chasing a false, distorted vision will cause you to quit and give up.** No one has a passion for something that is not theirs. *So, if you ever want to give up on your vision, you may want to re-examine whether it is really your vision or if it is someone else's.* If it is really yours, it should not be easy to let go. It is challenging to let go of something that belongs to you.

Failure Yields Success

Vision execution is challenging yet rewarding. It requires great effort and sacrifice. Almost every successful visionary will tell you that it was their failures that provoked their successes. Failures are stepping stones to success, and the two are inseparable. We may sometimes relate failure to finality because the thought of failure makes us feel hopeless and leads us to believe that what we so tirelessly worked for will never come to pass. When we pour out our heart, soul, and time into something and it fails, we tend to give up and move onto something else because we feel despondent and that time was wasted. That is so far from the truth. *Time exerted toward your vision is never misused but invested.* All investments are a gamble. However, one thing about investments is that eventually, there is a return. So, it is never a good idea to start executing your vision and then stop or give up because you had a setback or failure. Stop viewing failures as your enemy and start embracing them as teachable moments that will profit you in the long run. They are inevitable, and the only way to avoid failing is to stay dormant and do nothing.

Brian Tracy said it like this, **"*Failure is a prerequisite for great successes. If you want to succeed faster, double your rate of failure.*"** That simply means when you fail, get up and try and try again. The more you try, the more you may fail, but failure only gets you closer to the remedy for success.

Failure gives you the blueprint to what does not work so that you can discover what does. It helps you to revise your plan and change your approach. You will experience failures, but you must decide that failure is not your destiny, and quitting is not an option. Faith is walking out your vision without immediately seeing the full result. This reminds me of a story in the bible in the book of

Principle 8: Don't Give Up

Luke, chapter 18, that speaks of a widow who asked a judge to grant her justice against her adversary. After many attempts, the judge kept refusing her request, but finally, he granted her appeal due to her persistence. "NO" was not an option for her. She did not allow failure to hinder her. She never stopped believing that eventually, she would get what she desired. Therefore, her faith and persistence got her exactly what she envisioned.

> *Failure gives you the blueprint to what doesn't work so that you can discover what does.*

Now, look at some great visionaries who would not take "No" for an answer. They used their failures as fuel to drive them to success (Knatt, 2014).

Sylvester Stallone was rejected by talent scouts over 1500 times but kept trying. Eventually, he wrote "Rocky" and insisted that he star in the movie. Persistence secured him the part, and the rest is history. He is now worth approximately 400 million dollars. ***Stallone stated, "Every time I've failed, people had me out for the count, but I always come back."***

Stephen King, one of the most renowned authors in history, was rejected by 30 publishers before one of his writings was published. He would not give up and now has sold over 350 million books.

Joanne Rowling, the author of the Harry Potter series, took seven years to write Harry Potter, and 12 major publishers rejected it before it was finally accepted. She exercised persistence and has now sold over 450 million books and is one of the most successful authors of all time.

THE VISION BLUEPRINT

Colonel Sanders, the owner of Kentucky Fried Chicken, tried to sell his franchise chicken model and was rejected by over 1,000 restaurants before one accepted it. The franchise is one of America's most successful fast-food restaurants and now worth millions.

Michael Jordan, one of the world's greatest basketball players, was cut from his high school basketball team. He said, *"I have missed more than 9,000 shots in my career. I have lost almost 300 games. On 26 occasions I have been entrusted to take the game-winning shot, and I missed. I have failed over and over and over again in my life. And that is why I succeed. Obstacles don't have to stop you. If you run into a wall, don't turn around and give up. Figure out how to climb it, go through it, or work around it."*

> *"Failure is a prerequisite for great successes. If you want to succeed faster, double your rate of failure."*

Enough said! In other words, keep working on it and figure it out, but quitting is NOT an option.

Lastly, Thomas Edison, a renowned innovator and inventor, has almost 1100 patents. However, he failed over 10,000 times when trying to invent the light bulb. When asked how he failed numerous times, he commented, **"I have not failed 10,000 times. I have not failed once. I have succeeded in proving that those 10,000 ways will not work. When I have eliminated the ways that will not work, I will find the way that will work."**

So, in other words, where there is a will, there is a way. *If you can see success, then you can have success; but you can never have, or experience more than you can see.* You must be determined not to give up and continue to chase your vision until it is successfully

Principle 8: Don't Give Up

executed. When you are purposed and burdened to do something just like these visionaries, you cannot give up, and you will not give up. True vision will not let you be at peace doing something other than what you were created to do. If you find yourself being at peace with quitting, then that probably wasn't your vision. When it is truly your vision, no one or anything will be able to stop you from trying until you succeed.

You would probably say that Michael Jordan, Thomas Edison, and Colonel Sanders were crazy for trying over and over after failing thousands of times. I beg to differ; they would have been crazy not to keep trying. They had faith in what they saw and believed in it so much that quitting was not an option. Their vision dominated their very lives. They could not stop trying because they recognized that their vision was not about them. It was about impacting the lives of others who would reap the benefits of their faith, tenacity, and persevering spirit. Remember that your vision is never about you. It is about others who need what you have and about those who are depending on you not to quit so they can keep going.

One of the many valuable things that I learned in life is if you consistently practice anything, you will gradually improve at it and eventually master it. But you will not be able to do that if you start something, and when the going gets tough, you get going. You must stay there and keep working even when things look bad, when motivation is plummeting, people disappear, and money is low. Keep trying, no matter how it looks or feels, and decide and declare NOT to give up. *You must be determined to outlast your tears, fears, foes, roadblocks, and setbacks.*

When you are in a fight to fulfill your vision, either your opposition is going to wear you out, or you are going to wear it or them out. Decide to stand up again and again, even if you get knocked down over and over. The key is to take a breath, regroup, and dust yourself off, so you can get back in the game.

THE VISION BLUEPRINT

I watched the 2020 Louisiana State University (LSU) and Clemson University National College Championship game. Joe Burrow, LSU's star quarterback, was hit and hurt in the game several times, but I believe vision is what made him get back up each time. It was evident that he was determined to succeed and win the game no matter how many times he got knocked down. The agony of those hits showed all over his face. When asked if he was hurt even amid his undeniable pain, he shook it off. He said he was okay even though everyone could see that he was not. It was at that moment that he chose to exercise faith and persistence and not settle for defeat. His vision was to win the championship, and he knew the only way he could do that was to get back in the game.

The New Orleans Saints failed by losing at their first playoff game in 2020. However, they decided that they would not lodge in failure. Some of their final words were that they did not play their best game, but they would use their failures to prepare them for the next season. They understood that you win some and you lose some. They decided not to give up, but to get back in the game and work until they obtain victory.

When failure surprises you, use these recommendations and quotes to stay motivated.

- Take some "me" time to acknowledge what happened and heal.
- Remember that success proceeds failure.
  "Failure should be our teacher, not our undertaker.
  "Failure is delay, not defeat. It's a temporary detour, not a dead end. Failure is something we can avoid only by saying nothing, doing nothing, and being nothing."
  (Denis Waitley)
- Don't miss the lesson.
- Stay happy and optimistic and seek the good.
- Meditate on a solution and not the failure.
- Use failures to perfect your vision.

Principle 8: Don't Give Up

- Keep moving forward and choose not to accept failure.
- Revise your plan and strategize your comeback to combat the failure.
"Inaction breeds doubt and fear. Action breeds confidence and courage. If you want to conquer fear, don't sit at home and think about it. Go out and get busy." (Dale Carnegie)
- Remember others who failed but then succeeded.
- Remember your past failures and successes.
- Surround yourself with positivity and dismiss the negative.
- Stay focused and visualize your future success.

In summation, Ellen DeGeneres said it best, **"It's failure that gives you proper perspective on success."**

So, use failure to re-ignite the fire inside of you. Giving up on your vision indicates that you are giving up on yourself. If you don't believe that you will succeed, then no one else will. Getting back in the game while hurt and being wounded speaks volumes to your opponents and supporters. You must have the spirit of Arnold Schwarzenegger and let them know, *"I'm back"* when they counted you out. The more you attempt to do something, the more you will believe that you can do it. Consistently trying indicates that deep down inside, you know you can do it. If you did not think you could, you would not keep trying. You may get discouraged and fail, that is all a part of the blueprint, but you cannot stay discouraged. You must learn to encourage yourself when no one else is around. **Sometimes alone time forces grown time**. The quiet times create an atmosphere for self-reflection and transformation for growth. **Isolation brings about revelation, and revelation brings about clarification and illumination for your next success move**.

There are times when you will have to get by yourself to be reminded of your worth, of who God says you are, and of the gifts, talents, and abilities you have been given. You must remind yourself who you were created to be and what you were purposed to do. When you get discouraged, use this blueprint to revitalize yourself and get back on track. It is okay to take a step back to regroup and breathe when you fail, but it is not okay to reside there. Choose not to rest in failure and defeat, or you may become distracted and detour from the blueprint. Sometimes the remedy is for you to try a different strategy using the same blueprints. When facing failure, remind yourself that quitting is NOT an option. If Plan A fails, go to Plan B-Z and start all over again if you must, but NEVER quit trying.

> *"It's failure that gives you proper perspective on success." -Ellen DeGeneres*

When failure interrupts you, remind yourself that:

"I CAN DO THIS!"

"I AM A WINNER!"

"I AM VICTORIOUS!"

"FAILURE IS FUEL TO SUCCESS IN MY LIFE!"

"I WALK BY FAITH AND NOT BY SIGHT!"

"MY VISION WILL BE MANIFESTED!"

"MY VISION WILL WORK IF I CONTINUE TO WORK IT!"

"ALL I DO IS WIN NO MATTER WHAT!"

Principle 8: Don't Give Up

"NO," IS JUST ANOTHER WORD FOR "NEW OPPORTUNITIES!"

"THANKS, BE UNTO GOD WHO ALWAYS CAUSES ME TO TRIUMPH!"

"QUITTING IS NOT AN OPTION BECAUSE IT IS NOT IN MY BLOOD!"

Vow to It

You must be married to your vision. The sanctity of marriage involves a covenant and a commitment. A covenant is an agreement between two parties, and a commitment is a promise. You must make a verbal agreement with your vision to fulfill it 'til death do you part.' When you commit to something, you are dedicated to it. You are locked in, chained, and devoted to the cause. Commitment is defined as an engagement or obligation that restricts freedom of action ("Commitment," 2020). When you commit to something, that means that person or thing has your time, attention, passion, and love. It becomes a part of you, and it directs your actions. Committing implies that you have made a promise to do whatever it takes to bring it to fruition. It requires that you do what you need to do by any means necessary. Even when doing so means forsaking all else, working overtime, and sacrificing energy and money. Committing to your vision makes it a priority, and its completion is your mission. Commitment will make you keep trying because you are obligated to it. **Commitment and dedication bring fear to failure**. Together they inform failure that you are not afraid to fail, but you are afraid to quit. Commitment will push you as far as it takes to get you where you are trying to go. If you are fully committed, you cannot, and you will not stop because quitting is NOT an option!

THE VISION BLUEPRINT

> *You have to be married to your vision.*

Here are some important questions to help you see the benefits of failure and encourage you to understand the importance of not quitting but finishing.

Principle 8: Don't Give Up

REFLECTIONS

What are some failures that you have experienced?

What did you do to overcome those failures?

What can you do to overcome current failures?

What are some advantages/disadvantages of giving up?

What are the benefits of not giving up?

Where do you think you would be if you had not given up on your vision?

What or who motivates you from not giving up?

Today, I challenge you to reflect on your past failures and successes and to plan your next move toward executing or enhancing your vision. Please don't forget to ENJOY THE VISION JOURNEY.

THE VISION BLUEPRINT

PRAYER OF INSPIRATION

Lord, I ask that you remind me daily that I am a winner because of you. Remind me that you overcame every obstacle and adversary, therefore, so will I. Help me to remember that I can do all things through Christ that strengthens me. Remind me that I can accomplish anything through your power. Help me to vow to never take "No" for an answer. Help me to find ways to cross over every mountain, ride every wave, dodge every bullet, and finish every race. Help me to remember that you said when I go through the fire, it will not burn me, and if I go through the flood, it will not overtake me. Help me to remember that you are my way maker. Whenever it looks as if there is no way, remind me that you will make every crooked road straight and part the Red Sea just for me, if you must. Help me to vow never to give up on my passion, vision, and purpose. Help me to fulfill my destiny by any means necessary. Help me to stay committed to it. When failure visits me, help me to get up, dust myself off, and keep running until I cross the finish line. Help me to remember that the race is not given to the swift nor to the strong but to the one that endures to the end. Lord, help me to endure, execute my vision, and FINISH STRONG! When it's all said and done, help me to keep the faith and finish my course. Because my ultimate desire is to hear you say, "well done my good and faithful servant. In Jesus' name, Amen!

Visionary Corner

VISIONARY'S CORNER

Visionary's Corner

This information includes advice from various professionals in diverse industries and states. However, the one thing they all have in common is that they are all visionaries. They did not just write the vision, but they executed it. Utilize this tested, trusted information from these successful visionaries to catapult you into executing and enhancing your vision and living the life that you desire. I encourage you to use this blueprint, take their advice, and learn from their experiences. Follow their lead and change the narrative of your story to what you envisioned.

Jason Griffin - **IMR Athletics Sports Performance (Professional Sports Trainer)**

My vision was to create my own company and become a successful entrepreneur. I believed that if I was able to work for professional sports teams, then I could do it for myself. So, I say

Visionary Corner

the same to you. If you are using your gifts, talents, and abilities to bring someone else's vision to fruition and elevate someone else and their profit, then why can't you do it for yourself? I am a witness, and if I did it, then so can you. Invest in you just as much or more than you have invested into someone else. Work hard, and your vision will manifest.

Other advice:

- Don't be hesitant and fearful, but trust in God.
- Don't be afraid to fail. Without failure, there is no success.
- Always be willing to work on your craft daily.
- Be humble and listen and learn from others.
- Create a plan of action and be proactive in completing it.
- Research others who have successfully executed their vision.
- Be disciplined and focus on your vision daily.
- Never take "No" for an answer and Believe, Believe, Believe in yourself and your vision!!

Michael L. Smith - Imperial Essentials (all-natural multicultural growth and grooming beard care products)

The advice that I would give anyone who has a vision in mind is:

- Take a leap of faith.

- Start channeling and dedicating your thoughts and energy around that vision.

THE VISION BLUEPRINT

- Surround yourself with individuals who are successful and currently in the industry or field of interest of your vision.

- Write a plan and strategy for your vision so you can track your progress and achievements daily.

- Know how to handle losses and keep moving forward.

Other advice:

"Don't live your life with regret. Just do it."

"Don't let anything or anyone stop your drive."

"Create healthy outlets and a circle of encouragers."

"Always remember why you started."

Kwame Adkins - Southern U Properties/Subway Restaurants

I know from experience that it takes a great amount of courage and faith to step out of a box that you've been living in and pursue your God-given dreams!

Our instincts often kick in on purpose to give us a gut-feeling of caution. If you ever feel that way, ask God for guidance and direction, then step out in faith and act on what God tells you to do (or not do)!

I've learned that when you step out in faith, God has you firmly in the palm of His hand. If a door that you hoped to walk through has shut, trust that God has a better plan for you. If a door has opened that you are unsure of, trust that God will guide you along the way.

Below are strategies that I've learned along the way to fully execute my business plan.

- Set clear priorities.
- Collect and analyze your goals and data.
- Be consistent in our daily routine; repetition is crucial.
- Often evaluate your strategy to ensure its forward progression.

It's no secret that most businesses fail to deliver their intended results within the first five years of startup. The problem isn't normally the strategy but the way it's implemented. As business owners, we must often tweak our plans to ensure we spend our money wisely to increase our success.

I'm always encouraged to tell others who are chasing their dream to stay encouraged, believe in your product, and never be afraid to revisit your plan if it's not working in your favor.

I will leave you with this scripture. *"Now then, my sons, listen to me; blessed are those who keep my ways. Listen to my instruction and be wise; do not ignore it."* (Proverbs 8:32-33). In other words, pray and follow God's direction.

Spec McClendon – **Real Estate Owner**

- You must be whole, not broken or defective in order to successfully discover your purpose and execute your God-given vision. To be whole, you must love God completely

THE VISION BLUEPRINT

with all of your heart and mind. God is the creator and owner of us all. God is the glue and fabric that holds everything together.
- You need a team on this journey. The family unit is your team. God is the owner, you and your spouse are the coaches, and the rest of the family are your players. Your teammates are your partners in life.
- Start with your team and expand to others. True happiness begins with giving or helping others.

Other advice:

Material things and money come with hard work and dedication. Whatever you do to just get by, then double it. If you had someone working for you 30 or 40 hours a week and you got to keep their pay, would you hire them? Of course, you would, so hire yourself first. No one gets ahead working 30 hours a week. Most successful people work 60 to 80 hours per week, especially when they are just starting. So, choose a craft that you are passionate about because you will be spending a lot of time doing it.

Being completely whole, happy, and successful is not a goal that is hard to achieve. It only takes dedication to finish the race. Be patient, and you can be a millionaire before you know it. If I did it, so can you.

Troy Boutte – European Car Care

I had a fear of stepping out and owning my own business at first because it can be overwhelming. But if you truly want it, you will do whatever it takes to succeed and prosper. I encourage everyone to execute their vision because it affords you a sense of independence and ownership, which is an awesome, life-changing experience.

Other advice:

- Continue to grow in your business.
- Have a set salary, and never live on your business finances.
- Never allow other employees or anyone else to know more about your business than you.

Lloyd Ruffins – **Ruffin's Lounge and Ruffin's Event Center**

- Know your competition. Know where they are located and the scope of their products. Also, try to estimate future competitors as well.
- Do your research because the right location is vital to the success of your business.
- Start small and keep bills and overhead low until you build savings. Save, save, save.
- Don't get overconfident with quick success because things will level off at some point.
- Don't solely rely on anyone because people come and go.
- Be confident in yourself and your vision, keep working hard, and don't lose faith or give up, and you will succeed.

***Belinda Vining-Trepagnier* - Parishes Supportive Living, Inc.**

- Pray for your vision to be revealed and made clear and about what direction to go in. Make sure that you seek and see God in your vision before moving forward.
- Do your research to make sure there is a need for the service/business that you are providing.
- Know that you will make mistakes. I have been in business for over 19 years, and I still have a lot to learn.
- Always stay involved in your vision/business, even when it becomes successful.

***Dr. Mary Whitley Moss* - Senior Pastor - St. Alma Baptist Church of Lakeland, LA**

- Make sure you have a clear picture of what you think you see.
- Commit to what you "clearly" see.
- Though there may be moments of uncertainty, moments where there are more rough spots than you bargained for, moments when you are just plain tired, moments of discouragement when others can't see it, learn to trust God to bring your vision to pass.
- Finally, enjoy your journey!

Visionary Corner

Adrian Hammond - Boil and Roux Restaurant

"Work every day like it's your first day." In other words, work hard, learn from your successes and failures, and don't ever give up.

Dima Ghawi, LLC. **- Leadership Keynote Speaker and Executive Coach**

My intuition guided me to start my business. I had a calling to do something bigger than I am and create a lasting change in the world. Five years ago, I resigned from my job at IBM and embarked on my journey as a leadership speaker and executive coach. There is a need for people to get the guidance required for professional advancement, and I wanted to be able to fully focus my time on helping my clients expand their potential.

I would assure those fearful of executing their vision that feeling afraid is normal. We all experience it, and that fear will always be there. You can choose to let that fear control you or utilize the fear to motivate you into growth. When starting my business, I was propelled by the fear of looking back and wishing that I had done something differently. Now, these emotions have helped me to share my leadership journey with the world.

THE VISION BLUEPRINT

Tips to execute your vision:

- If you have something calling you to work on a new or challenging project, this means you have a bigger purpose than you may imagine. Trust in your intuition and the guidance that you are receiving because there is a reason for your calling.
- Always think about how your work will make a difference in the lives of others. You are not alone. There are individuals who will be influenced by your work, and that is a blessing.
- Recognize that there are always going to be wins and situations where we don't win. Do not mull over these negatives as failures; instead, think of them as a learning opportunity to grow and get better.

Bobby Russell - **The Dungeon Gym**

In order to pursue your vision, you can't allow your mind to dictate to you who you are. Your mind needs to be transformed by the daily reading of God's Word. Control your thoughts with the Word of God. Believe what God said about you. Don't allow the world to tell you who you are. See yourself the way God sees you. The Bible declares in Romans 12:2, "And be not conformed to the world: but, be ye transformed by the renewing of your mind, that ye may prove what is that good and acceptable and perfect will of God."

Seek God's Word and will for your life, and:

- Learn your identity.
- Learn what belongs to you.

- Learn the authority you have in Jesus.
- Learn how to walk in the authority of God's Will concerning you.
- Learn to walk by faith and live the blessed life that God has for you.

Dr. Antoinette Harrell - Historian, Genealogist, Author, and Filmmaker

I was diagnosed with a Giant Cell Tumor of the bone, and I spent five years recovering. I was unable to seek employment during those years. Self-employment was the only way I could manage to provide for my family. Fear of failure wasn't an option. I decided if it didn't work the first time, I wasn't going to give up. *My advice to you is*:

- Pray and trust God. If He placed a vision inside of you, He will guide you all the way.
- Surround yourself with people who have accomplished what you're trying to accomplish.
- Write down your goals and the formula for achieving that goal. Read it daily and repeat it out loud. What helped me to achieve my goals was writing down my daily tasks every evening, so I knew what my tasks were for the next day, week, and month.
- Develop a strategy, mission, and purpose. Now it's time to execute your vision.
- Do not be afraid to make mistakes along the way. Please understand that in the mistakes, you will learn some valuable lessons and pay close attention to those lessons.

THE VISION BLUEPRINT

- Purchase books on the subject, attend seminars, and, most importantly, seek a mentor who can help you develop your vision.
- Walk with confidence and see yourself having accomplished your vision before you see it in the natural. In other words, have faith in God and yourself.

Lisa Brown - **Assisted Hands** (Long-term adult care) and **Kreative Minds** (child and geriatric behavioral and mental health care agency)

My desire to start these agencies was my vision to see people given the guidance they need to draw on their own strengths and realize their true potential to live a fulfilling, happy life, physically and mentally.

Starting anything new is a challenge, but you have to step out in faith and research what it is that you desire to do. *You must*:

- Connect yourself with people with positive mindsets and people who will help you accomplish what you're trying to accomplish.
- Stay focused and work daily. Sometimes you have to step back to regroup and revitalize yourself but giving up is never an option.
- Revisit your vision and business plan to encourage yourself. Never stop learning and growing in the midst of your success.
- Believe in yourself, do the work, and remember that anything is possible and obtainable.

Visionary Corner

Andre Scott - **ACH Builders**

My vision was birthed 15 years ago, while I was searching for a way to secure retirement for my family. I started with rental property and moved to homebuilding. Real estate is the safest vehicle to create long term wealth.

When executing your vision, research and education are key. I educated myself for two years before I made my first investment.

Unfortunately, today we live in a microwave society that's guided by fear. Meaning, our culture tells us you can get rich quick without any risk. This is not true; you have to take risks to get rich. Your vision should always be centered around God's purpose and plan for your life. My advice to you is to pray for God's wisdom and guidance because "Men give advice, but God gives guidance."

There is no burden heavier than an unfulfilled potential. Step out in faith, educate yourself, pray, and connect with other vision-minded individuals. "If you don't build your vision, then someone will hire you to help build theirs.

"Vision without EXECUTION is hallucination."

Thomas Edison

REFERENCES

Accenture 2013 Global Consumer Pulse Survey. Global and U.S. Key Findings. Retrieved from https://www.accenture.com/t20150523t052453__w__/us-en/_acnmedia/accenture/conversion-assets/dotcom/documents/global/pdf/strategy_3/accenture-global-consumer-pulse-research-study-2013-key-findings.

Arogyalokesh, V. (2020). What is CKM? Retrieved from https://mindmajix.com/what-is-crm

Buchel, M. (2019, June). Tyler Perry: Rags to Riches. *The Importa Magazine*, Retrieved from https://theimportamagazine.com/tyler-perry-rags-to-riches/

D'Angelo, M. (2019, January). "Small Business Solutions and Inspiration: 6 Things to do Before Starting a Business." *Business Daily News*, Retrieved from https://www.businessnewsdaily.com/1484-starting-a-business.html

Ducille, M. (2020). You Can Begin Again. *Called Magazine*, Retrieved from https://www.calledmagazine.com/magazine-articles/inspiration/item/130-cover-story-joyce-meyer?start=0

Heath, T. (2018, August). Apple is the first $1 trillion company in history. *The Washington Post*, Retrieved from https://www.washingtonpost.com/business/economy/apple-is-the-first-1-trillion-company-in-history/2018/08/02/ea3e7a02-9599-11e8-a679-b09212fb69c2_story.html

Identity. (2020). In *Merriam-Webster Dictionary*. Retrieved from https://www.merriam-webster.com/dictionary/identity. Accessed 3 May. 2020.

Insanity. (2020). In *Merriam-Webster Dictionary*. Retrieved from https://www.merriam-webster.com/dictionary/insanity. Accessed 3 May. 2020

Kahneman, D. (2011). Thinking Fast and Slow. Details, Research and Decision-Making Process. Farrar, Straus and Giroux, LLC. Publishing.

Knatt, R. (2014). 48 Famous Failures Who Will Inspire You to Achieve [Blog post]. Retrieved from https://www.wanderlustworker.com/48-famous-failures-who-will-inspire-you-to-achieve.

Levesque, R.J.R. (2001). In Encyclopedia of Adolescence. Ego Identity.

New King James Version. (1982). BibleGateway.com. https://www.biblegateway.com/versions/New-King-James-Version-NKJV-Bible/

Process. (2020). In *Oxford Dictionary*. Retrieved from https://www.lexico.com/en/definition/process.

Spaeder, K.E. (2020, January 4). How to Research Your Business Idea. Retrieved from https://www.entrepreneur.com/article/70518.

Quarter 3 (2018). The Nielsen Total Audience Report: Share of Time Spent by Platform.

Self-worth. (2020). In *Dictionary.com*. Retrieved from https://www.dictionary.com/browse/self-worth?s=t. 2020.

U. S. Small Business Administration. Write Your Business Plan. https://www.sba.gov/about-sba/open-government/about-sbagov-website/social-media

Vision. (2020). In *Oxford Dictionary*. Retrieved from https://www.lexico.com/en/definition/vision

Visionary (2020). In *Merriam-Webster.com Dictionary*. Retrieved from https://www.merriam-webster.com/dictionary/visionary#:~:text=(Entry%201%20of%202)nature%20of%20a%20vision%20%3A%20illusory

The White House Office of Consumer Affairs.

www.ingramcontent.com/pod-product-compliance
Lightning Source LLC
Chambersburg PA
CBHW071006160426
43193CB00012B/1942